twenty 21

January

S	M	T	W	T	F	S
					1	2
3	4	5	6	7	8	9
10	11	12	13	14	15	16
17	18	19	20	21	22	23
24	25	26	27	28	29	30
31						

February

S	M	T	W	T	F	S
	1	2	3	4	5	6
7	8	9	10	11	12	13
14	15	16	17	18	19	20
21	22	23	24	25	26	27
28						

March

S	M	T	W	T	F	S
	1	2	3	4	5	6
7	8	9	10	11	12	13
14	15	16	17	18	19	20
21	22	23	24	25	26	27
28	29	30	31			

April

S	M	T	W	T	F	S
				1	2	3
4	5	6	7	8	9	10
11	12	13	14	15	16	17
18	19	20	21	22	23	24
25	26	27	28	29	30	

May

S	M	T	W	T	F	S
						1
2	3	4	5	6	7	8
9	10	11	12	13	14	15
16	17	18	19	20	21	22
23	24	25	26	27	28	29
30	31					

June

S	M	T	W	T	F	S
		1	2	3	4	5
6	7	8	9	10	11	12
13	14	15	16	17	18	19
20	21	22	23	24	25	26
27	28	29	30			

July

S	M	T	W	T	F	S
				1	2	3
4	5	6	7	8	9	10
11	12	13	14	15	16	17
18	19	20	21	22	23	24
25	26	27	28	29	30	31

August

S	M	T	W	T	F	S
1	2	3	4	5	6	7
8	9	10	11	12	13	14
15	16	17	18	19	20	21
22	23	24	25	26	27	28
29	30	31				

September

S	M	T	W	T	F	S
			1	2	3	4
5	6	7	8	9	10	11
12	13	14	15	16	17	18
19	20	21	22	23	24	25
26	27	28	29	30		

October

S	M	T	W	T	F	S
					1	2
3	4	5	6	7	8	9
10	11	12	13	14	15	16
17	18	19	20	21	22	23
24	25	26	27	28	29	30
31						

November

S	M	T	W	T	F	S
	1	2	3	4	5	6
7	8	9	10	11	12	13
14	15	16	17	18	19	20
21	22	23	24	25	26	27
28	29	30				

December

S	M	T	W	T	F	S
			1	2	3	4
5	6	7	8	9	10	11
12	13	14	15	16	17	18
19	20	21	22	23	24	25
26	27	28	29	30	31	

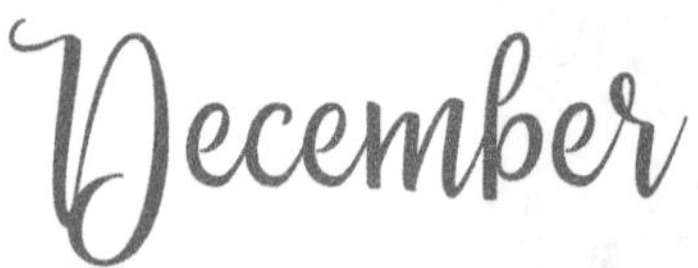

December 2020

SUNDAY	MONDAY	TUESDAY	WEDNESDAY
		1	2
6	7	8	9
13	14	15	16
20	21 First Day of Winter (Winter Solstice)	22	23
27	28	29	30

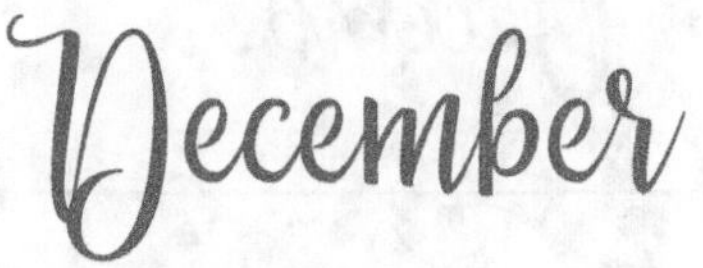

December

2020

THURSDAY	FRIDAY	SATURDAY	NOTES
3	4	5	○
			○
			○
			○
			○
10 Hanukkah Begins	11	12	○
			○
			○
			○
17	18 Hanukkah Ends	19	○
			○
			○
			○
24 Christmas Eve	25 Christmas Day	26	○
			○
			○
			○
			○
31 New Year's Eve			NOTES

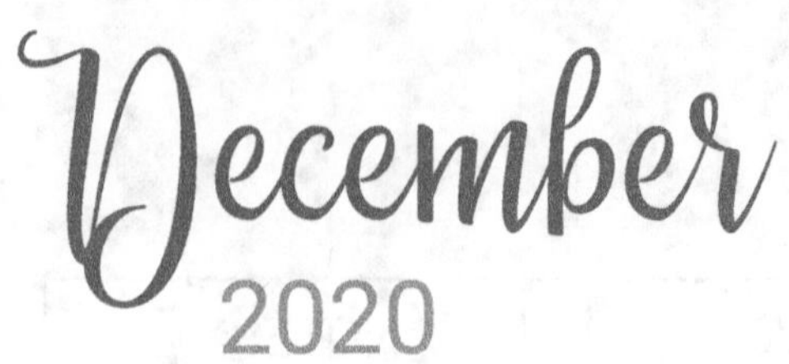

December
2020

30 MONDAY

01 TUESDAY

02 WEDNESDAY

03 THURSDAY

04 FRIDAY

05 SATURDAY

06 SUNDAY

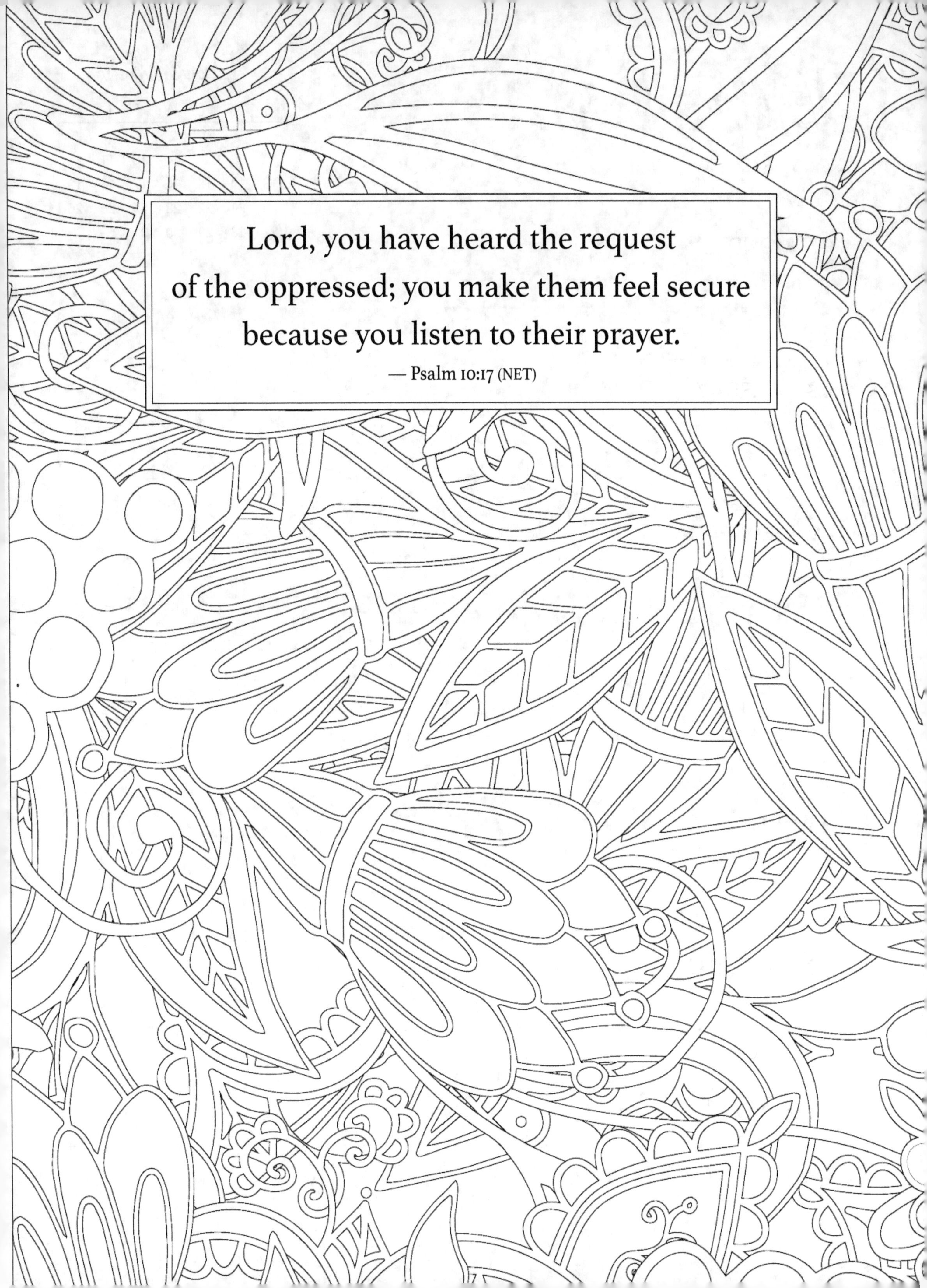

Lord, you have heard the request
of the oppressed; you make them feel secure
because you listen to their prayer.

— Psalm 10:17 (NET)

December
2020

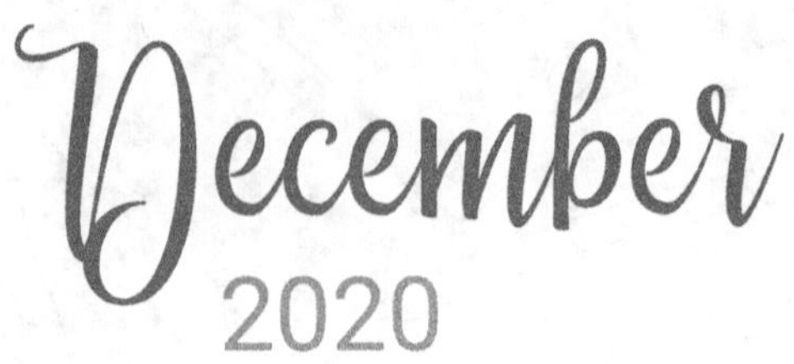

07 MONDAY

08 TUESDAY

09 WEDNESDAY

10 THURSDAY Hanukkah Begins

11 FRIDAY

12 SATURDAY

13 SUNDAY

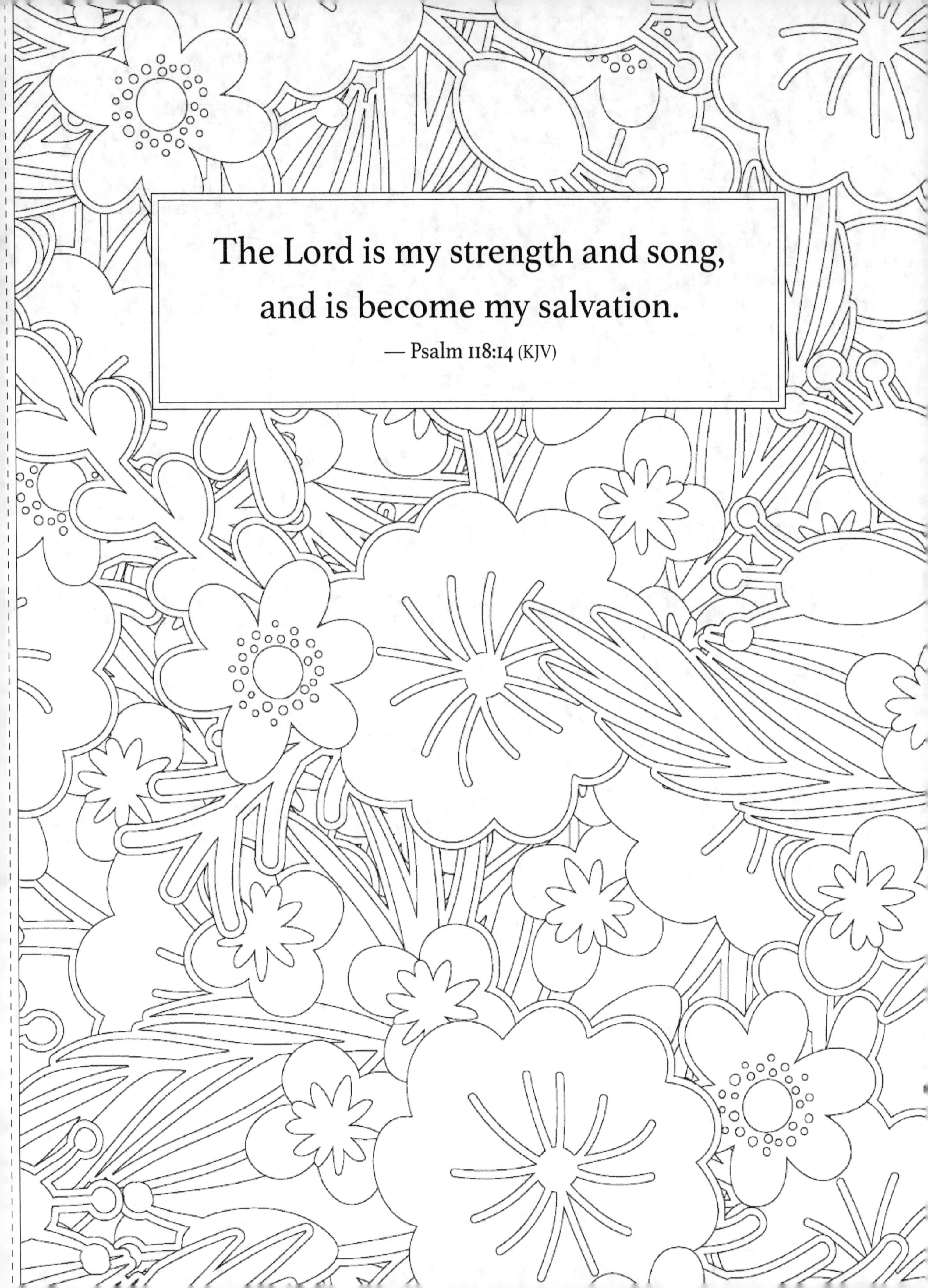

The Lord is my strength and song,
and is become my salvation.
— Psalm 118:14 (KJV)

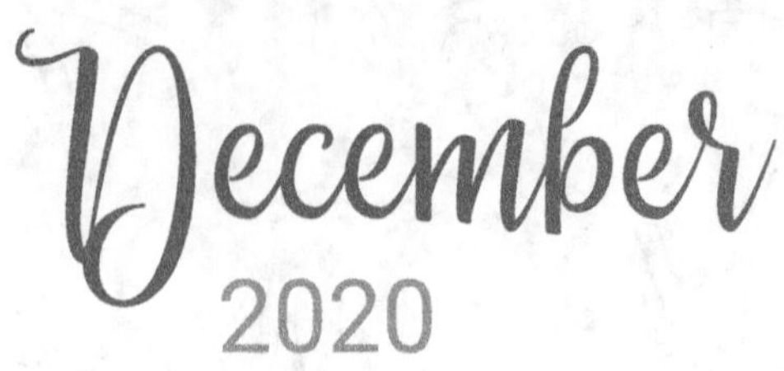

December
2020

14 MONDAY

15 TUESDAY

16 WEDNESDAY

17 THURSDAY

18 FRIDAY Hanukkah Ends

19 SATURDAY

20 SUNDAY

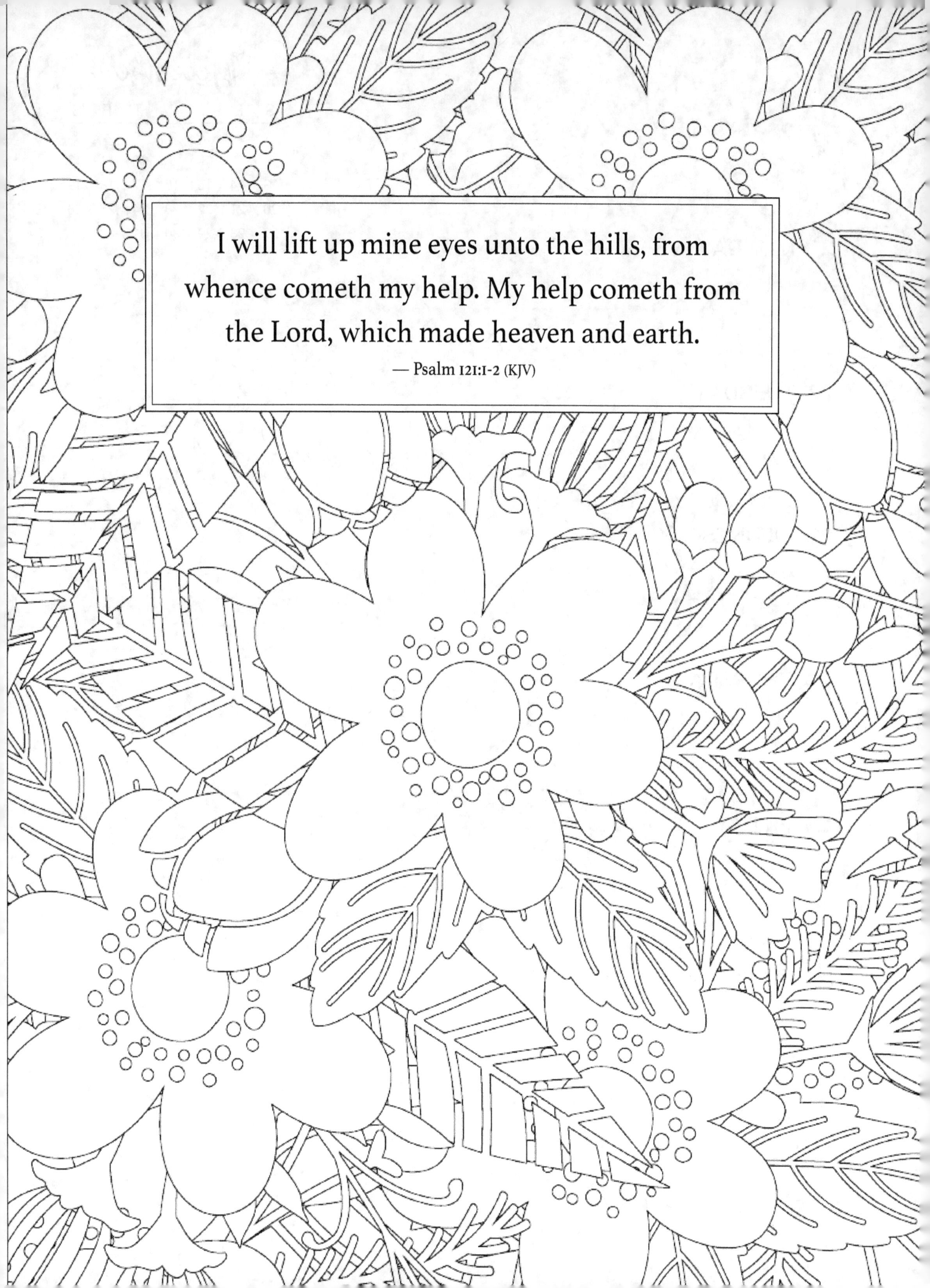

I will lift up mine eyes unto the hills, from whence cometh my help. My help cometh from the Lord, which made heaven and earth.

— Psalm 121:1-2 (KJV)

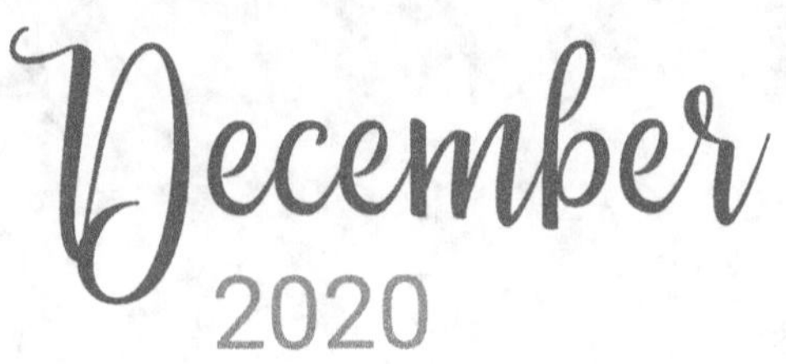

December
2020

21 MONDAY   First Day of Winter (Winter Solstice)

22 TUESDAY

23 WEDNESDAY

24 THURSDAY   Christmas Eve

25 FRIDAY   Christmas Day

26 SATURDAY

27 SUNDAY

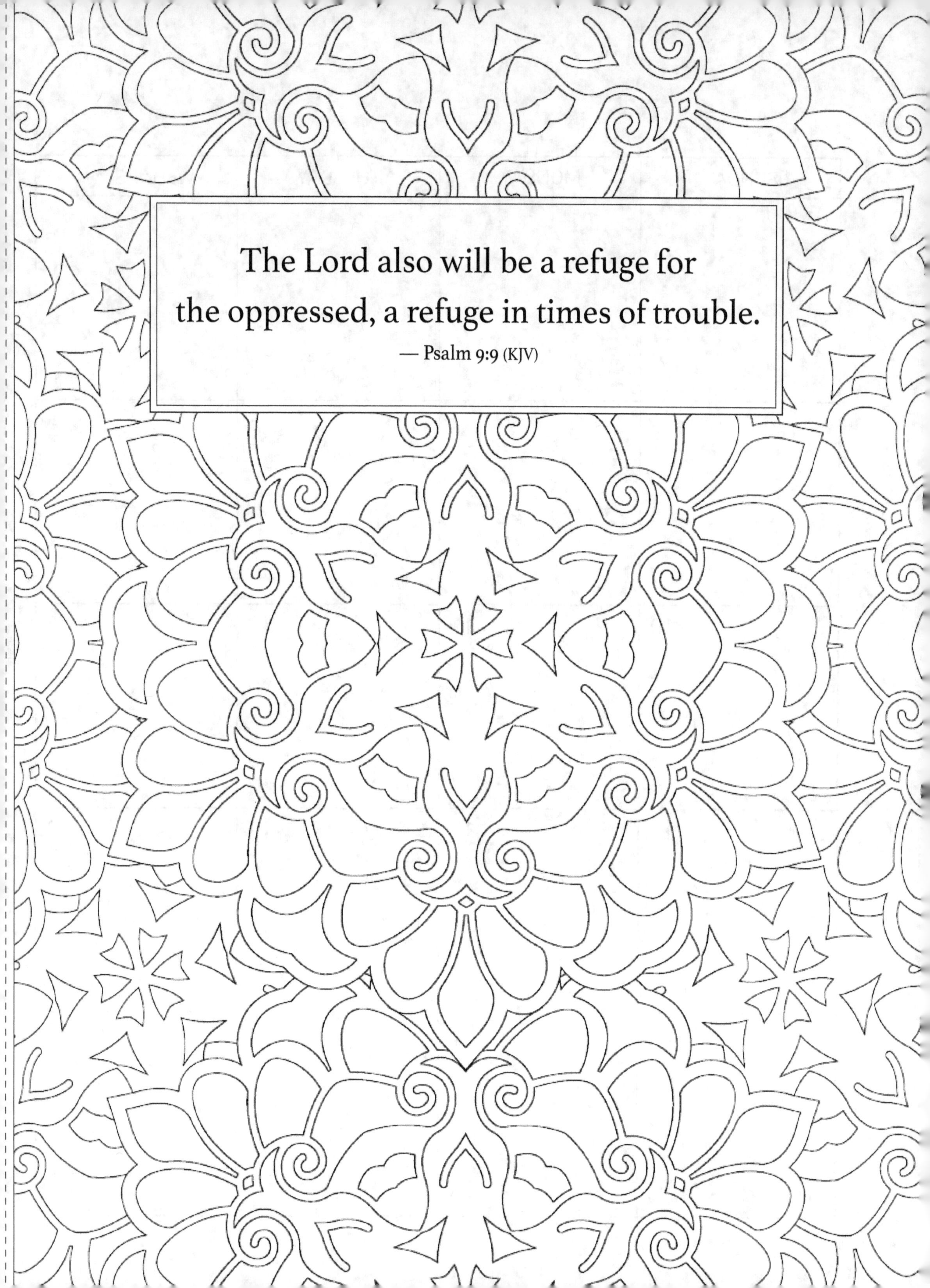

The Lord also will be a refuge for
the oppressed, a refuge in times of trouble.
— Psalm 9:9 (KJV)

January

2021

SUNDAY	MONDAY	TUESDAY	WEDNESDAY
3	4	5	6
10	11	12	13
17	18 Martin Luther King Jr. Day	19	20
24 31	25	26	27

January 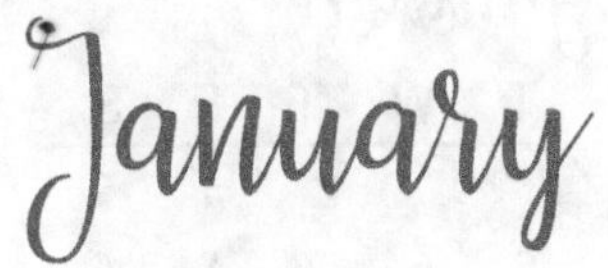 2021

THURSDAY	FRIDAY	SATURDAY	NOTES
	1 New Year's Day	2	○
			○
			○
			○
			○
7	8	9	○
			○
			○
			○
14	15	16	○
			○
			○
			○
21	22	23	○
			○
			○
			○
			○
28	29	30	NOTES

January
2021

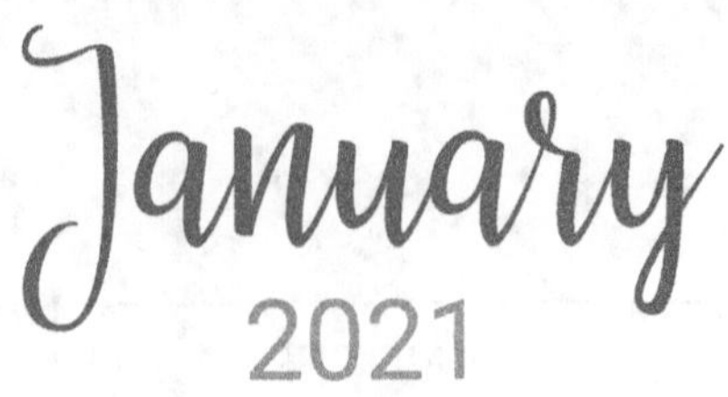

28 MONDAY

29 TUESDAY

30 WEDNESDAY

31 THURSDAY   New Year's Eve

01 FRIDAY   New Year's Day

02 SATURDAY

03 SUNDAY

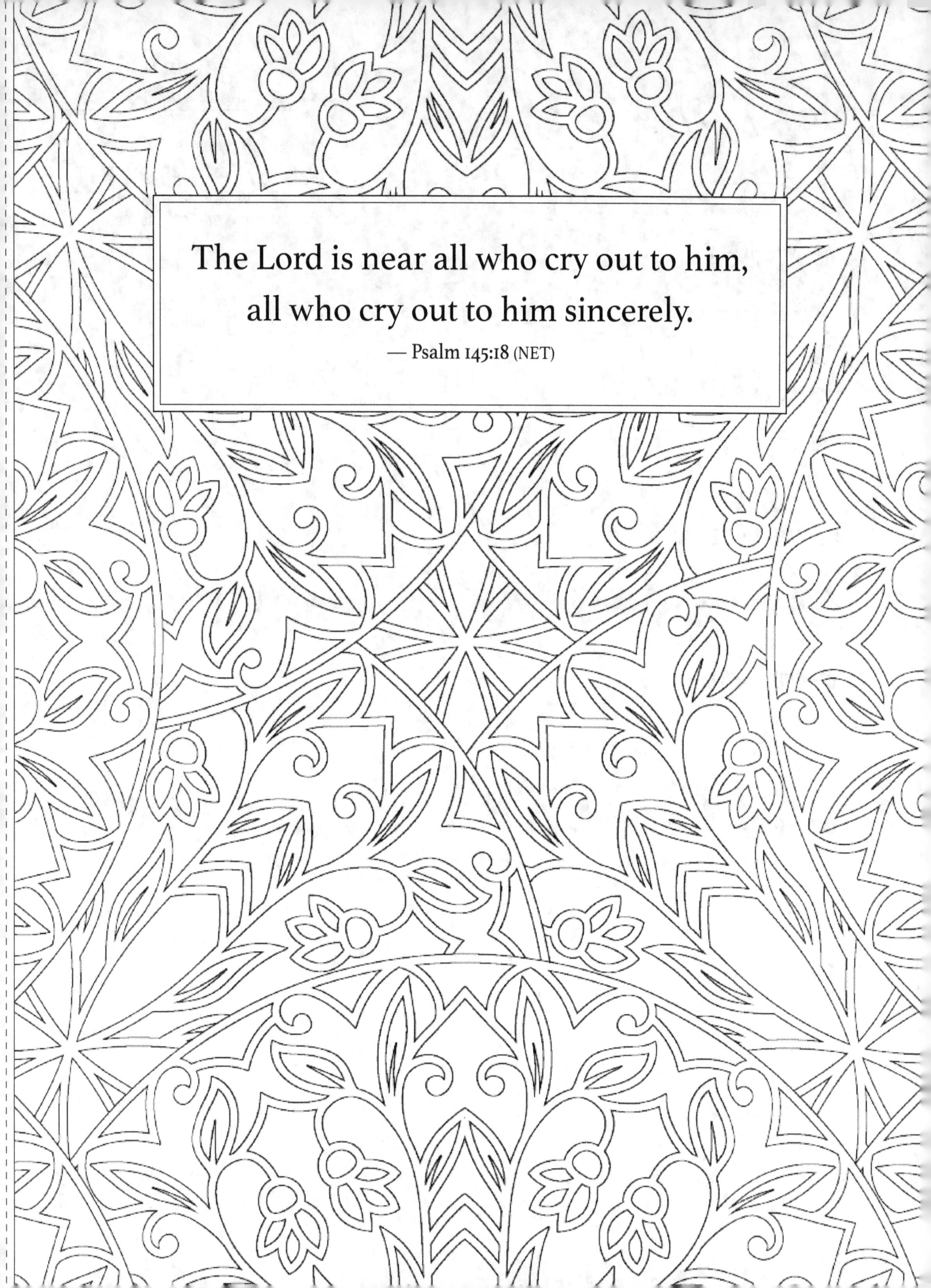

The Lord is near all who cry out to him,
all who cry out to him sincerely.
— Psalm 145:18 (NET)

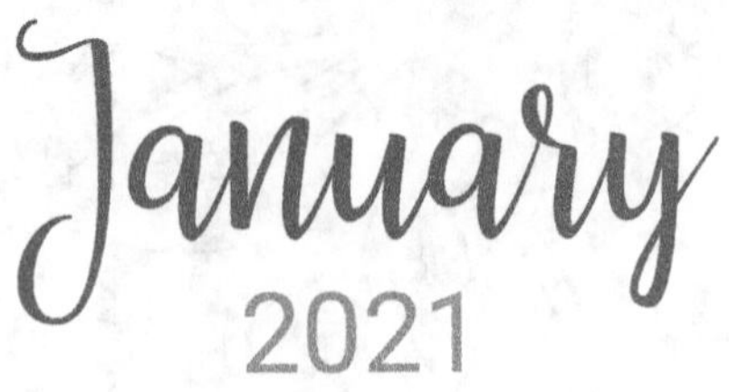

January
2021

04 MONDAY

05 TUESDAY

06 WEDNESDAY

07 THURSDAY

08 FRIDAY

09 SATURDAY

10 SUNDAY

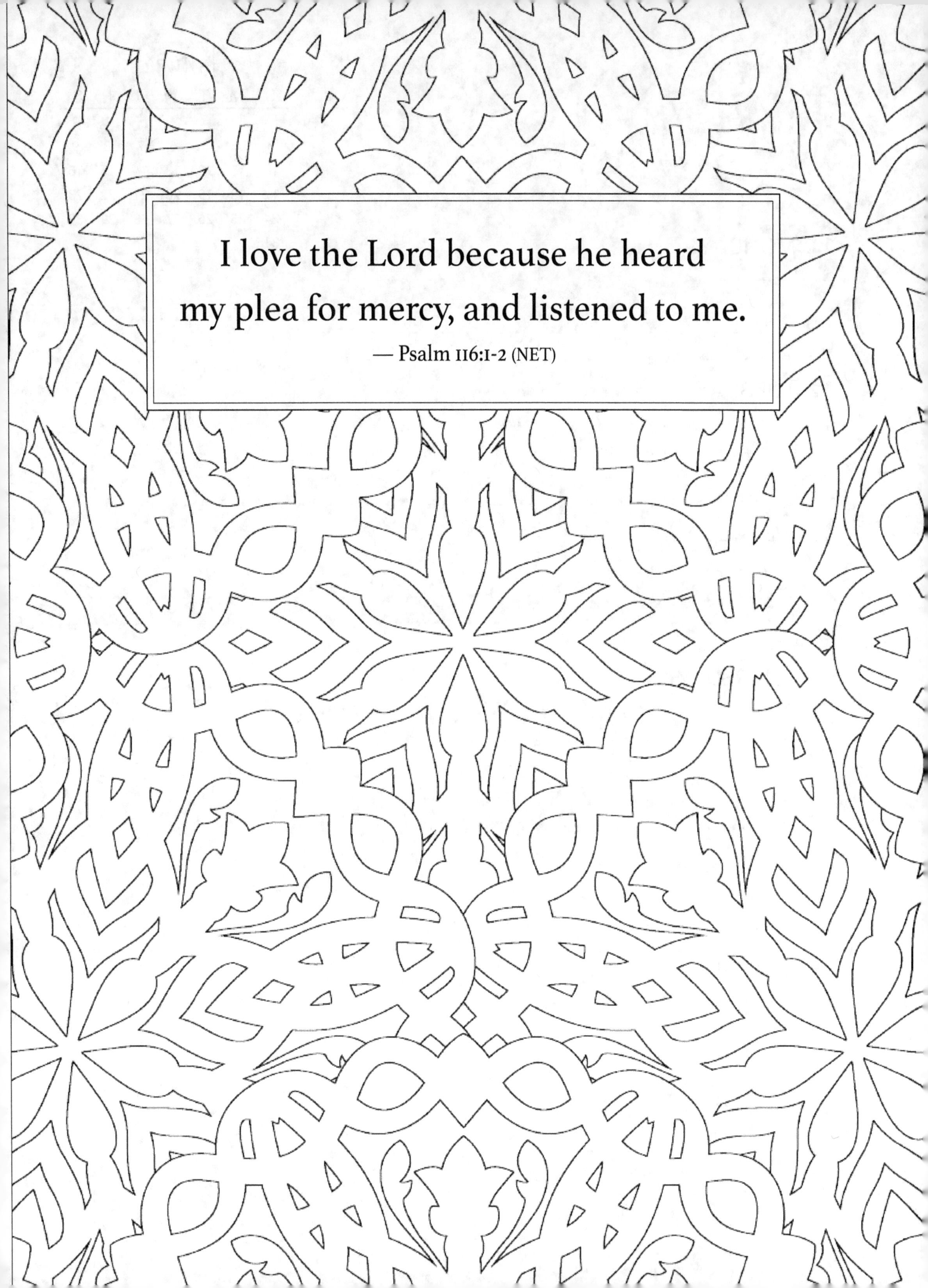

I love the Lord because he heard
my plea for mercy, and listened to me.
— Psalm 116:1-2 (NET)

January
2021

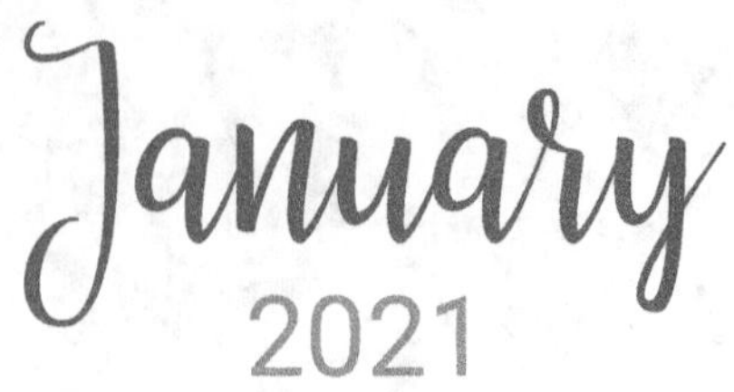

11 MONDAY

12 TUESDAY

13 WEDNESDAY

14 THURSDAY

15 FRIDAY

16 SATURDAY

17 SUNDAY

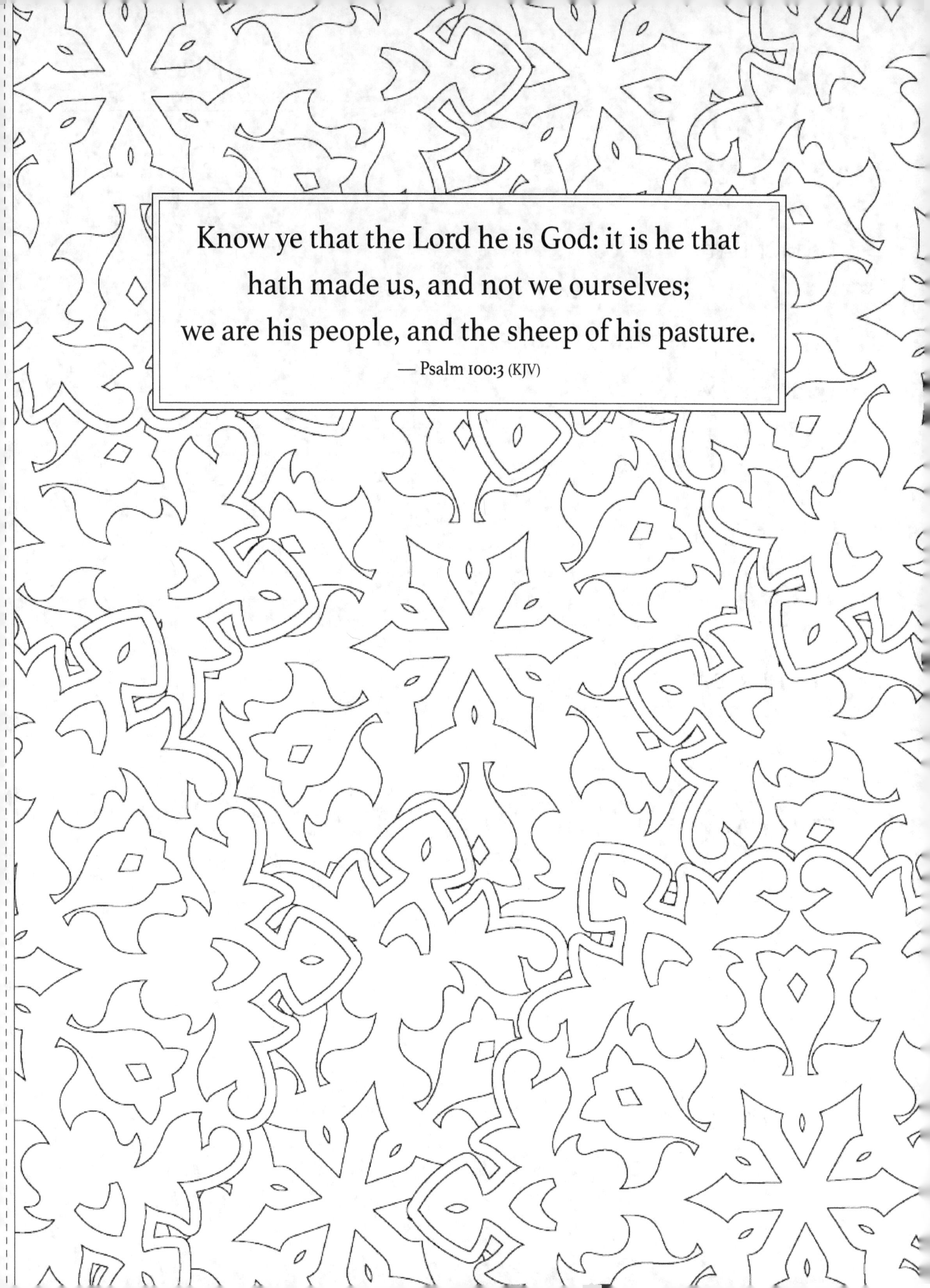
Know ye that the Lord he is God: it is he that
hath made us, and not we ourselves;
we are his people, and the sheep of his pasture.
— Psalm 100:3 (KJV)

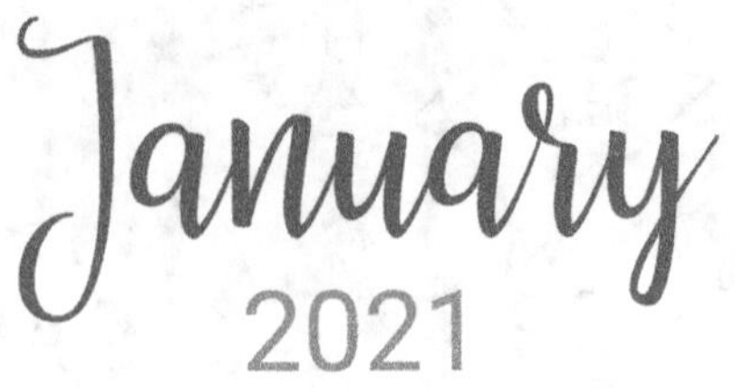

January
2021

18 MONDAY · Martin Luther King Jr. Day

19 TUESDAY

20 WEDNESDAY

21 THURSDAY

22 FRIDAY

23 SATURDAY

24 SUNDAY

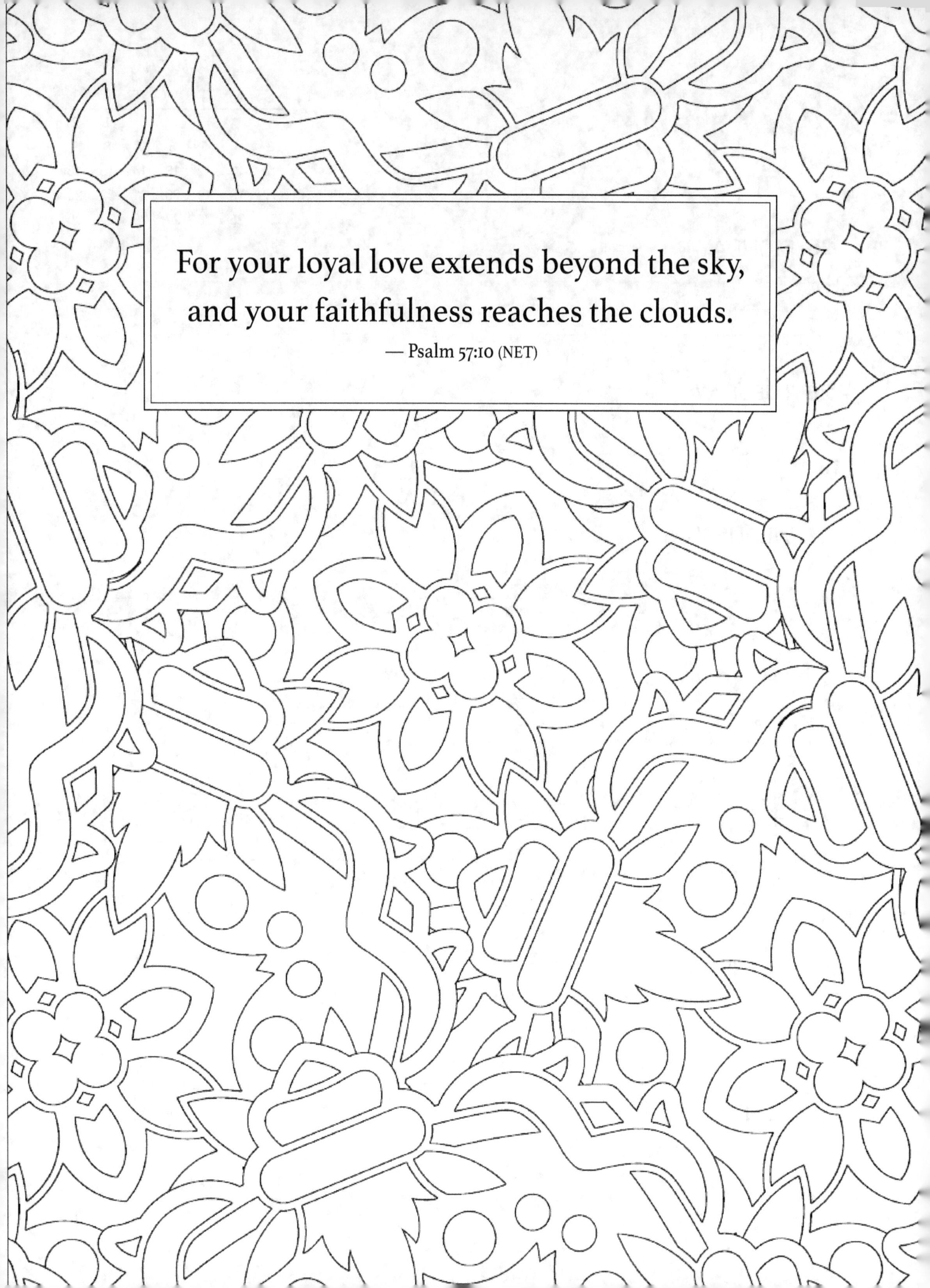

For your loyal love extends beyond the sky,
and your faithfulness reaches the clouds.
— Psalm 57:10 (NET)

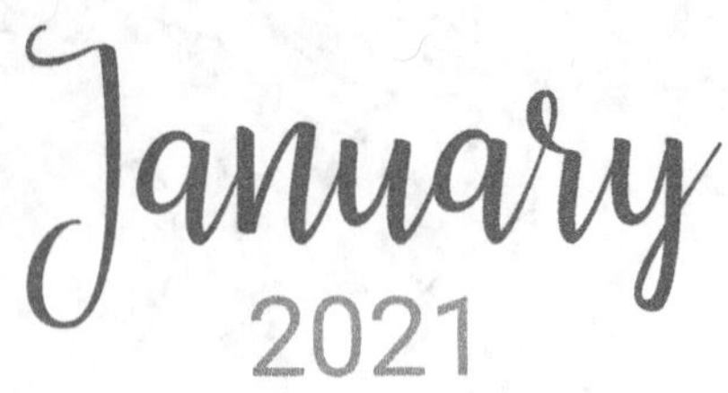

25 MONDAY

26 TUESDAY

27 WEDNESDAY

28 THURSDAY

29 FRIDAY

30 SATURDAY

31 SUNDAY

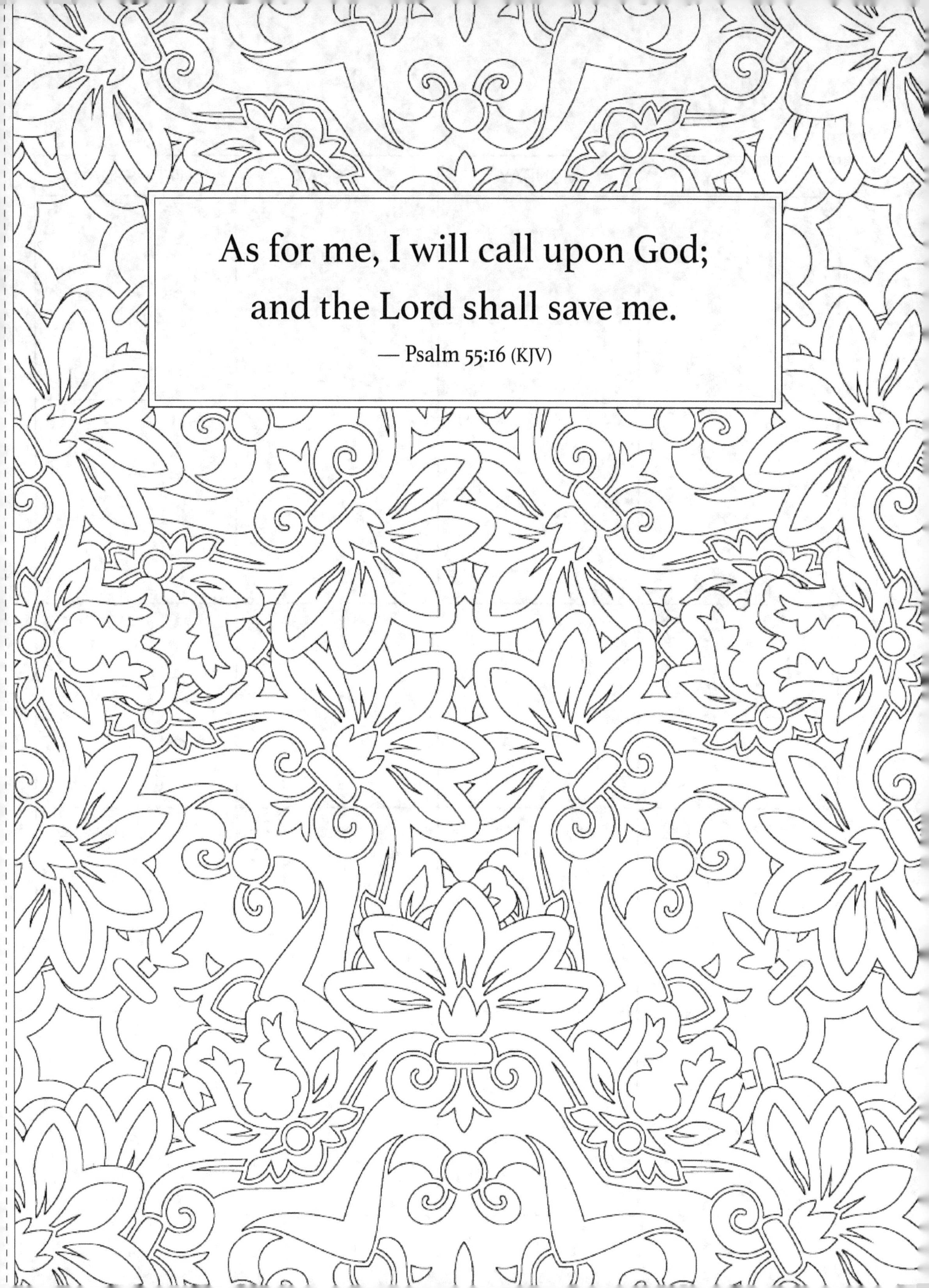

As for me, I will call upon God;
and the Lord shall save me.
— Psalm 55:16 (KJV)

SUNDAY	MONDAY	TUESDAY	WEDNESDAY
	1	2	3
7	8	9	10
14 Valentine's Day	15 President's Day	16	17
21	22	23	24
28			

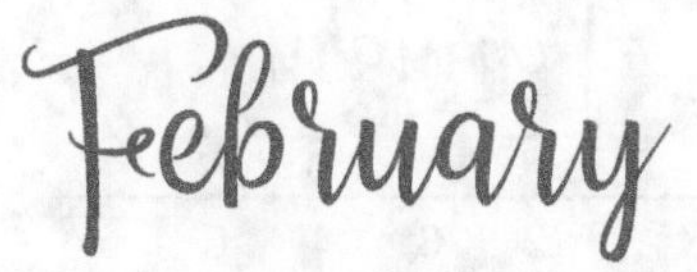

February 2021

THURSDAY	FRIDAY	SATURDAY	NOTES
4	5	6	○
			○
			○
			○
			○
11	12	13	○
			○
			○
			○
18	19	20	○
			○
			○
			○
			○
25	26	27	○
			○
			○
			○
			○
			NOTES

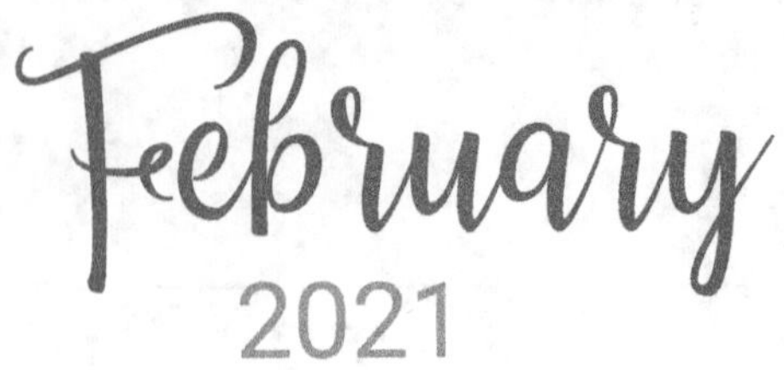

February
2021

<table>
<tr><td colspan="7">February</td></tr>
<tr><td>S</td><td>M</td><td>T</td><td>W</td><td>T</td><td>F</td><td>S</td></tr>
<tr><td></td><td>1</td><td>2</td><td>3</td><td>4</td><td>5</td><td>6</td></tr>
<tr><td>7</td><td>8</td><td>9</td><td>10</td><td>11</td><td>12</td><td>13</td></tr>
<tr><td>14</td><td>15</td><td>16</td><td>17</td><td>18</td><td>19</td><td>20</td></tr>
<tr><td>21</td><td>22</td><td>23</td><td>24</td><td>25</td><td>26</td><td>27</td></tr>
<tr><td>28</td><td></td><td></td><td></td><td></td><td></td><td></td></tr>
</table>

01 MONDAY

02 TUESDAY

03 WEDNESDAY

04 THURSDAY

05 FRIDAY

06 SATURDAY

07 SUNDAY

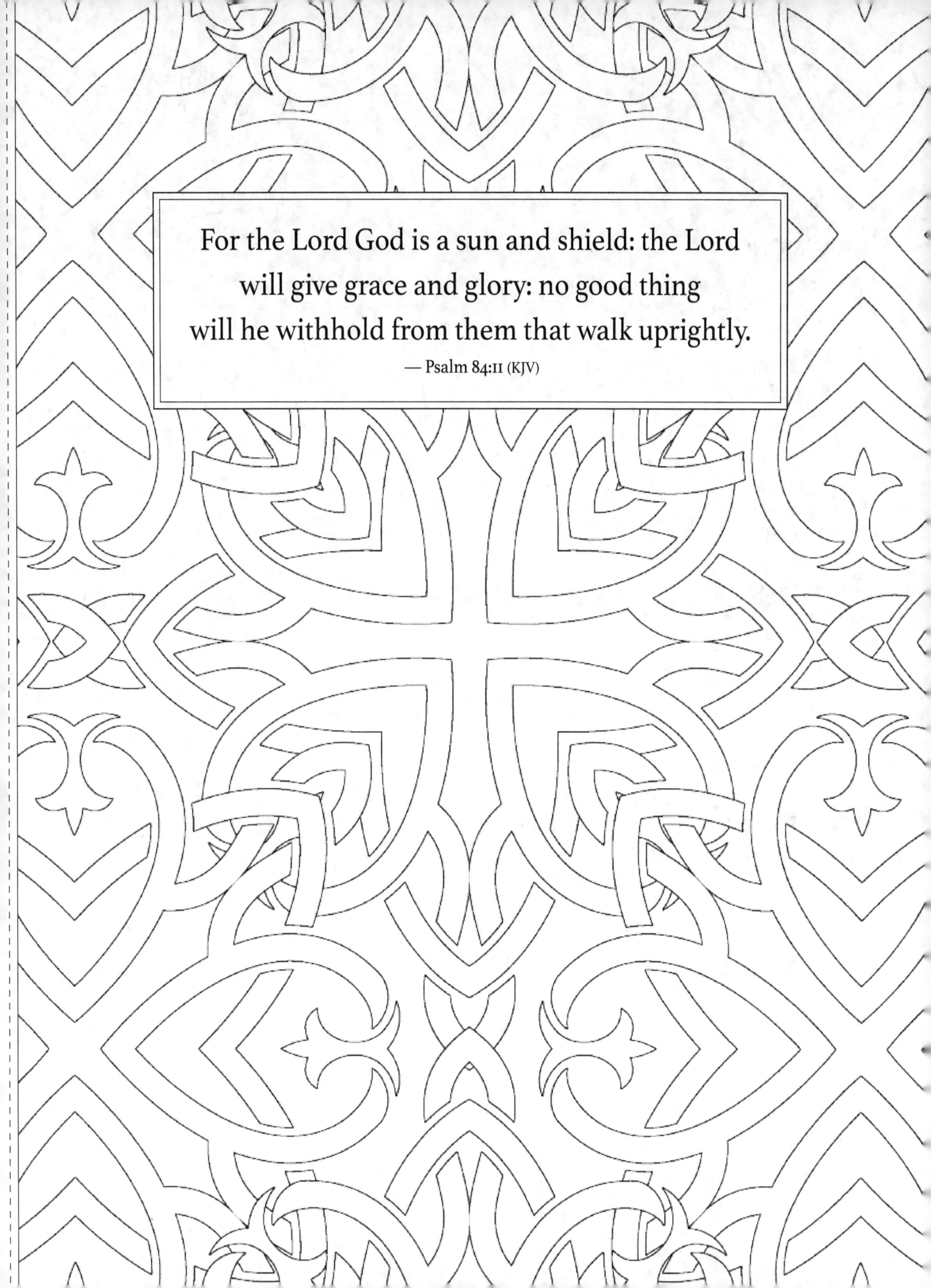
For the Lord God is a sun and shield: the Lord
will give grace and glory: no good thing
will he withhold from them that walk uprightly.
— Psalm 84:11 (KJV)

February
2021

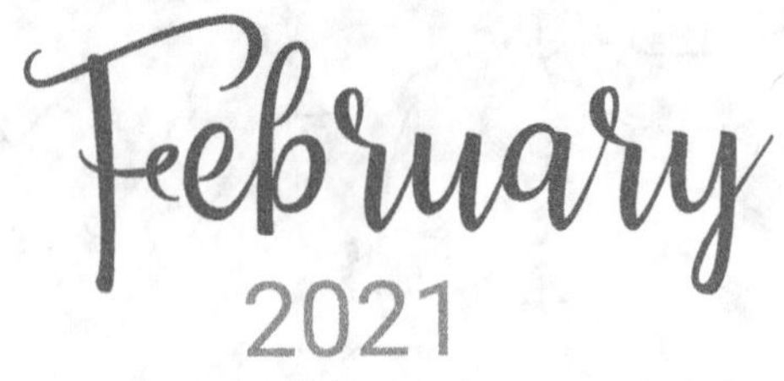

08 MONDAY

09 TUESDAY

10 WEDNESDAY

11 THURSDAY

12 FRIDAY

13 SATURDAY

14 SUNDAY Valentine's Day

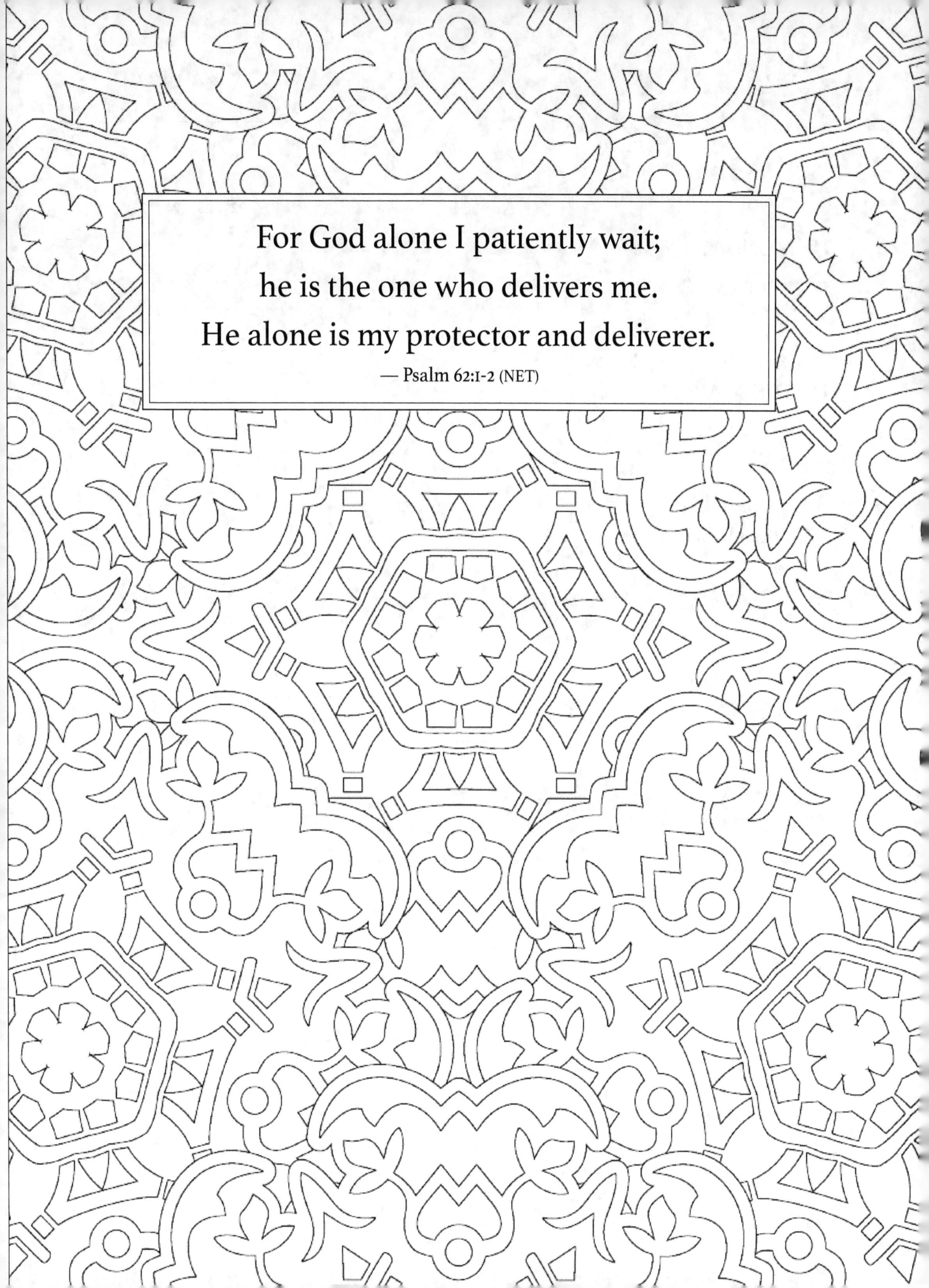

For God alone I patiently wait;
he is the one who delivers me.
He alone is my protector and deliverer.
— Psalm 62:1-2 (NET)

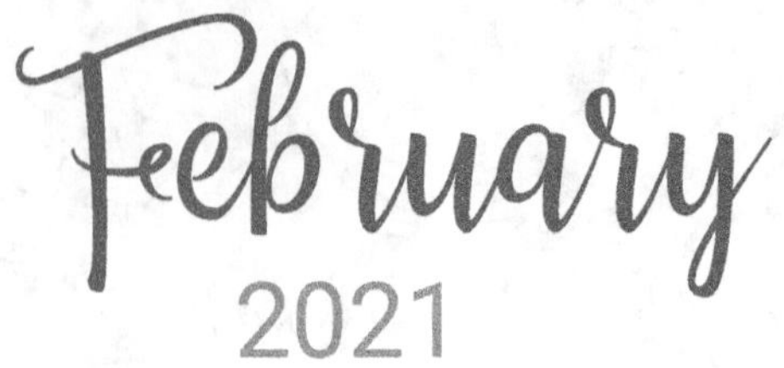

February
2021

15 MONDAY   President's Day

16 TUESDAY

17 WEDNESDAY

18 THURSDAY

19 FRIDAY

20 SATURDAY

21 SUNDAY

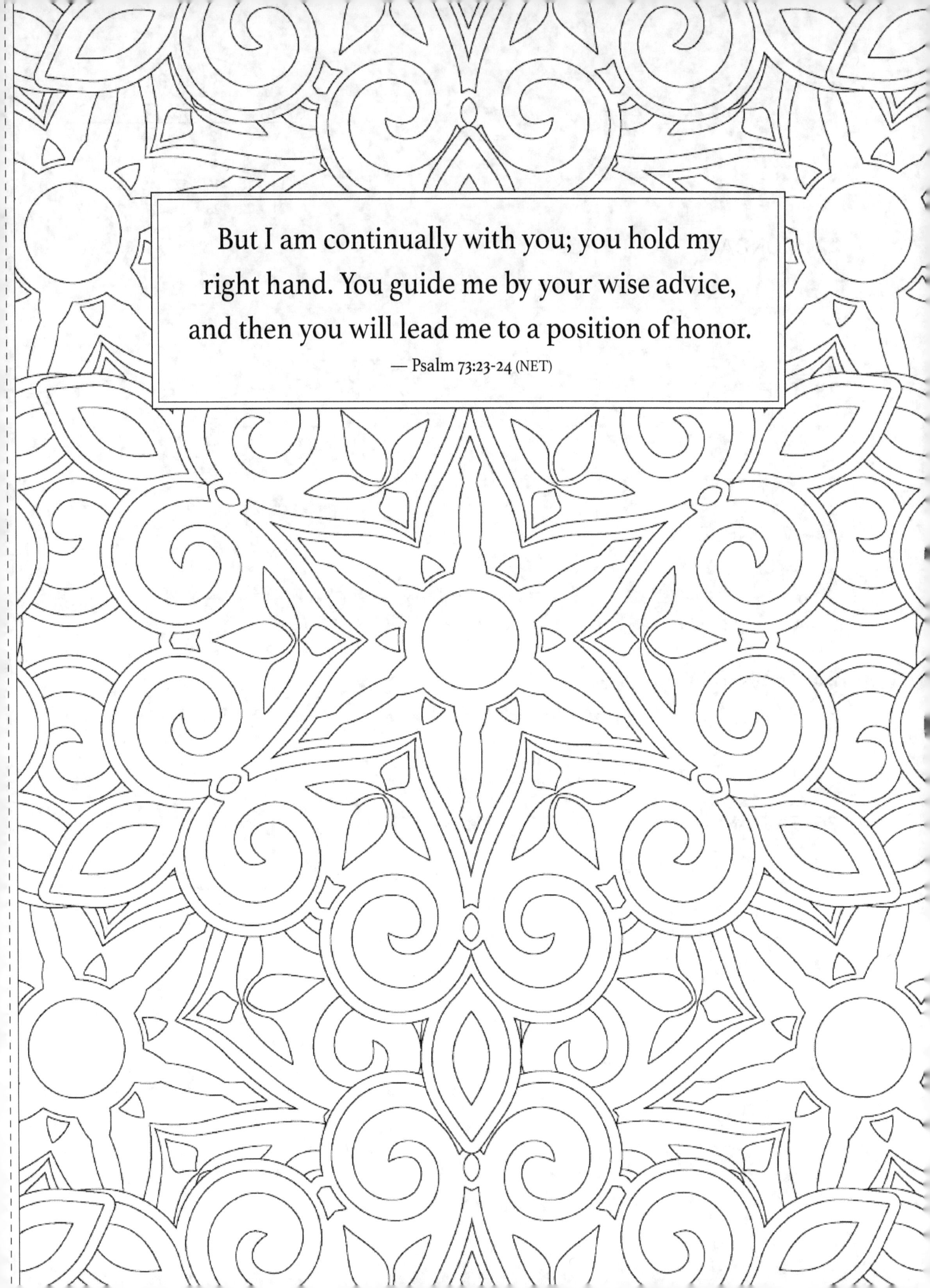

But I am continually with you; you hold my
right hand. You guide me by your wise advice,
and then you will lead me to a position of honor.
— Psalm 73:23-24 (NET)

February
2021

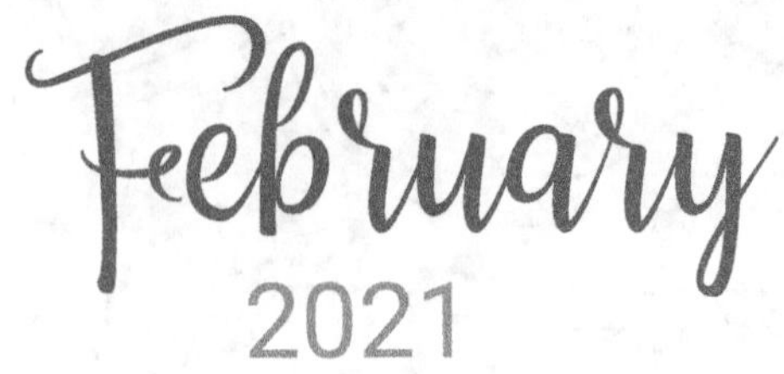

22 MONDAY

23 TUESDAY

24 WEDNESDAY

25 THURSDAY

26 FRIDAY

27 SATURDAY

28 SUNDAY

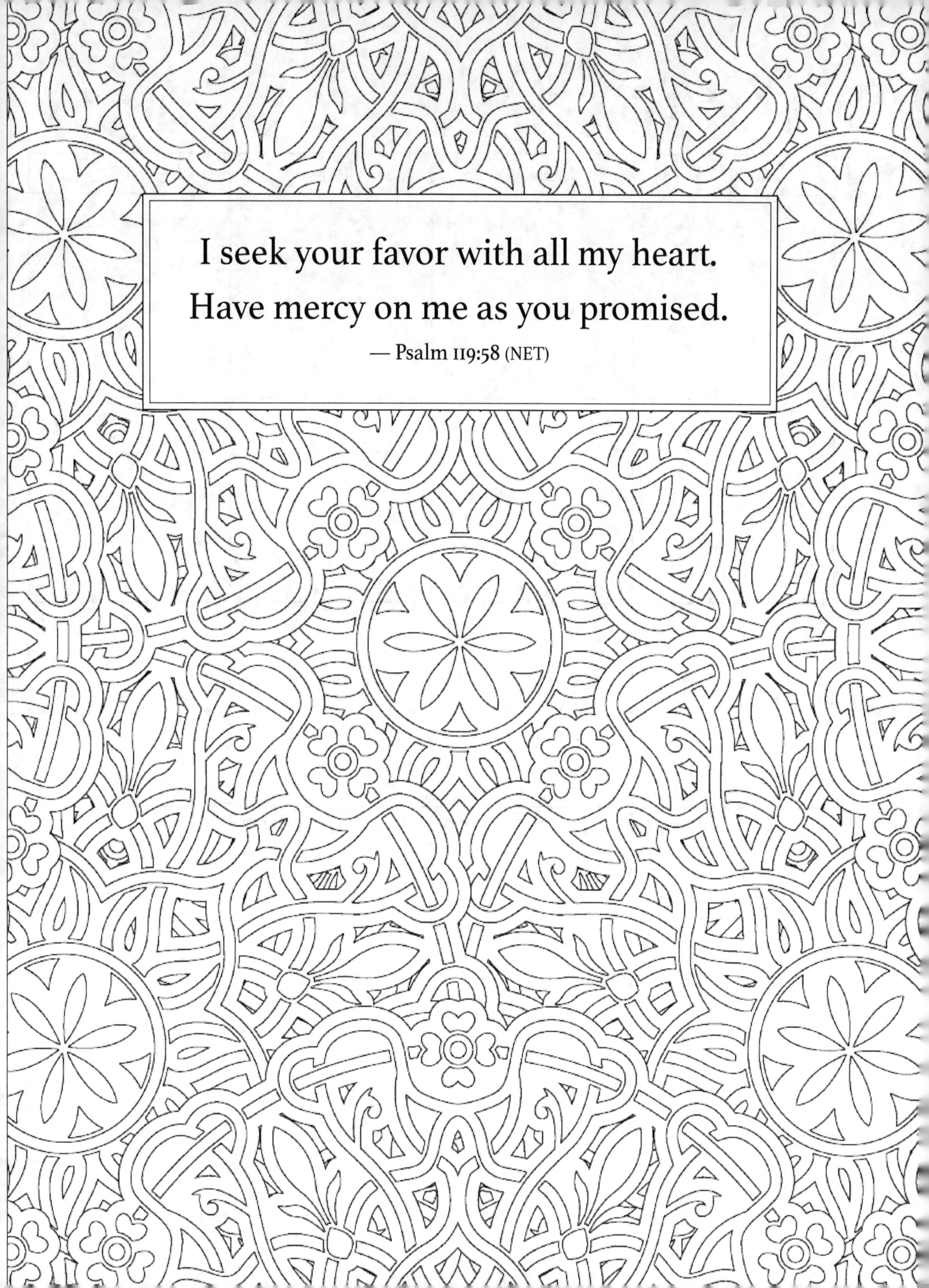

I seek your favor with all my heart.
Have mercy on me as you promised.
— Psalm 119:58 (NET)

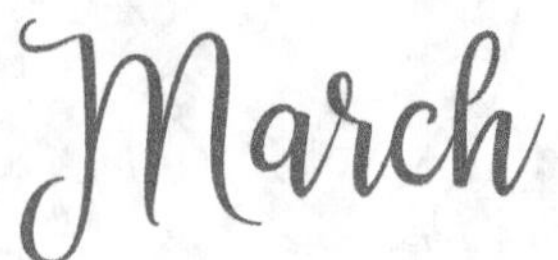

March

2021

SUNDAY	MONDAY	TUESDAY	WEDNESDAY
	1	2	3
7	8	9	10
14 Daylight Savings Time Begins	15	16	17
21	22	23	24
28	29	30	31

March 2021

THURSDAY	FRIDAY	SATURDAY	NOTES
4	5	6	○
			○
			○
			○
			○
11	12	13	○
			○
			○
			○
18	19	20 First Day of Spring	○
			○
			○
			○
25	26	27 Passover Begins	○
			○
			○
			○
			○
			NOTES

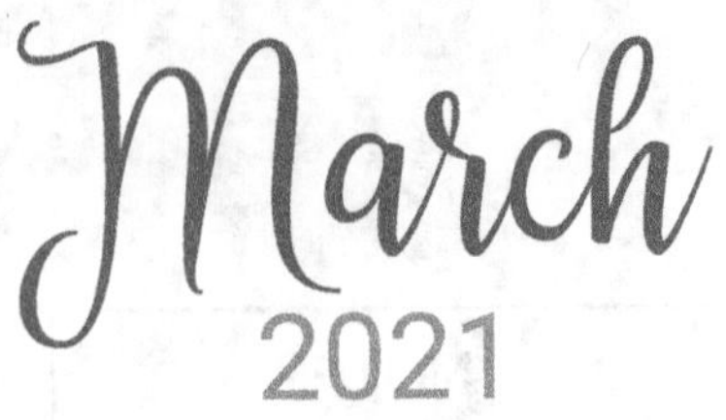

March
2021

01 MONDAY

02 TUESDAY

03 WEDNESDAY

04 THURSDAY

05 FRIDAY

06 SATURDAY

07 SUNDAY

When I said, My foot slippeth;
thy mercy, O Lord, held me up.
— Psalm 94:18 (KJV)

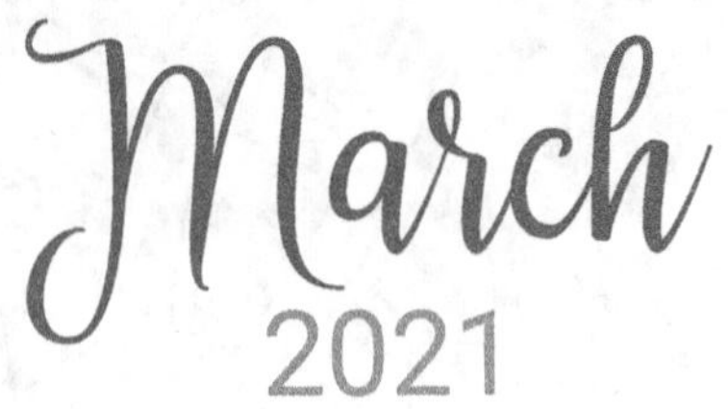

March
2021

March

S	M	T	W	T	F	S
	1	2	3	4	5	6
7	8	9	10	11	12	13
14	15	16	17	18	19	20
21	22	23	24	25	26	27
28	29	30	31			

08 MONDAY

09 TUESDAY

10 WEDNESDAY

11 THURSDAY

12 FRIDAY

13 SATURDAY

14 SUNDAY   Daylight Savings Time Begins

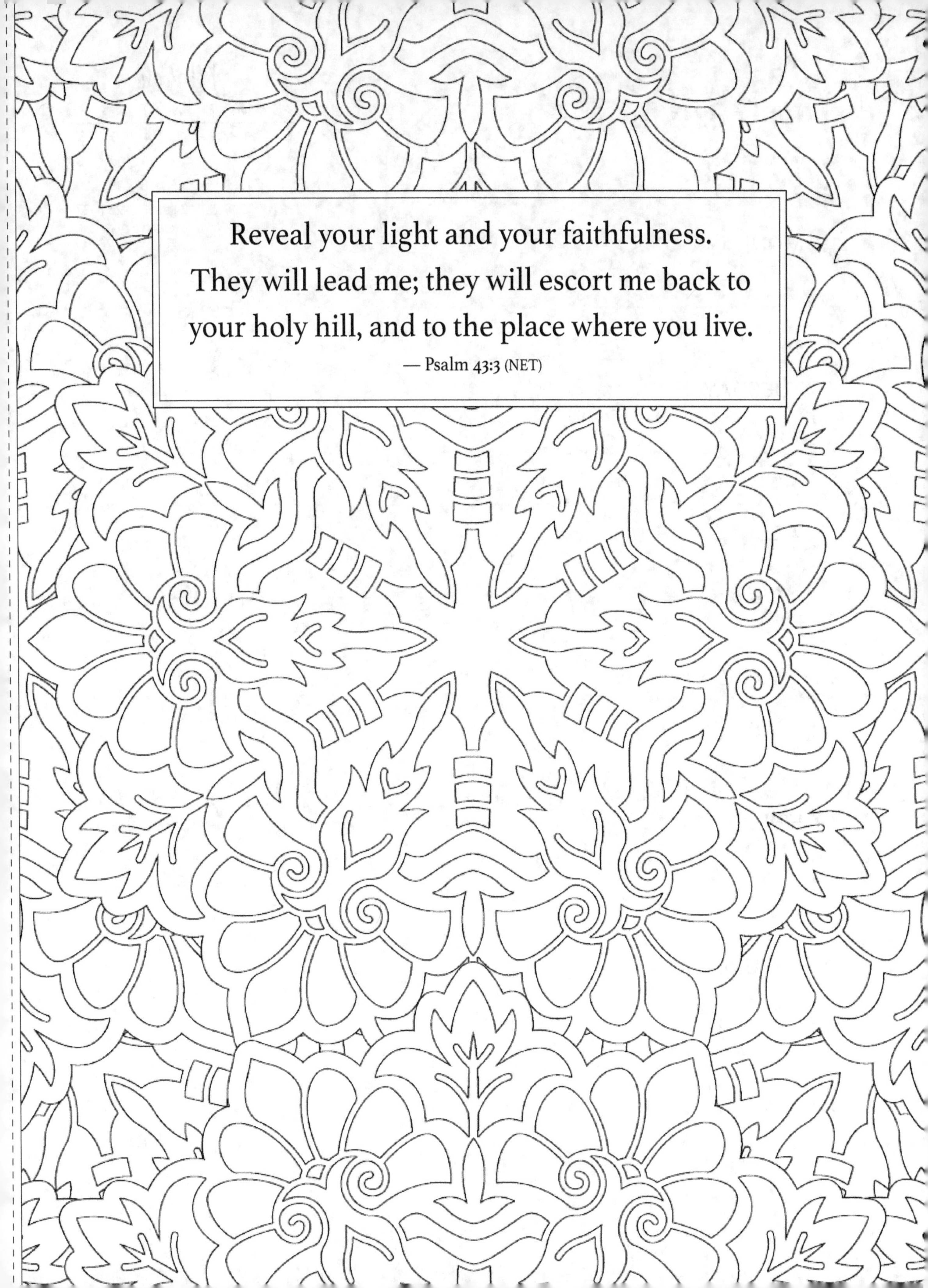

Reveal your light and your faithfulness.
They will lead me; they will escort me back to
your holy hill, and to the place where you live.
— Psalm 43:3 (NET)

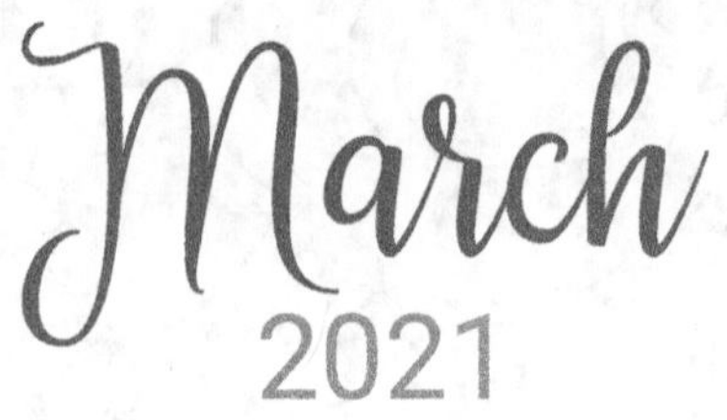

March 2021

15 MONDAY

16 TUESDAY

17 WEDNESDAY   St. Patrick's Day

18 THURSDAY

19 FRIDAY

20 SATURDAY   First Day of Spring

21 SUNDAY

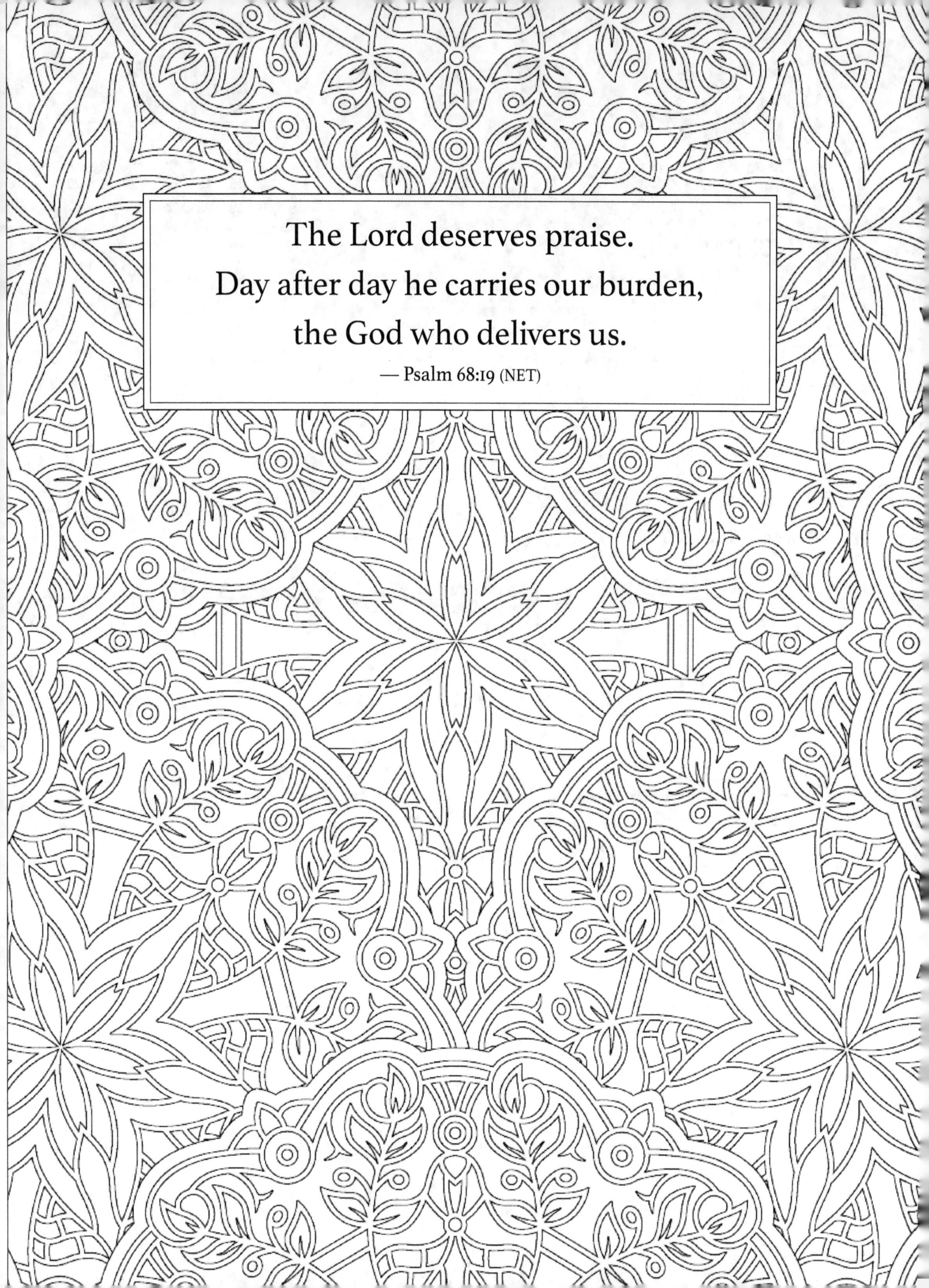

The Lord deserves praise.
Day after day he carries our burden,
the God who delivers us.
— Psalm 68:19 (NET)

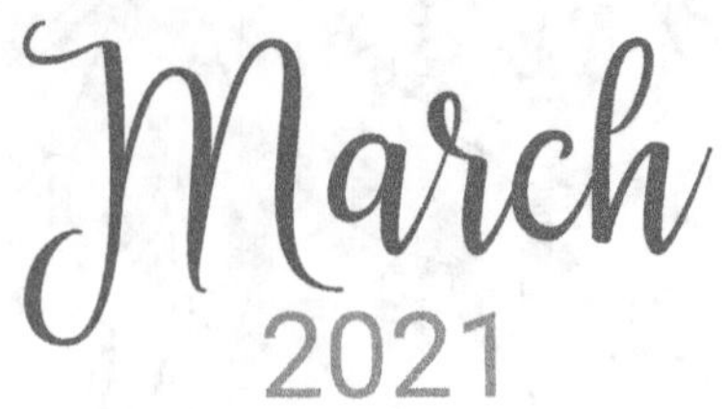

March
2021

22 MONDAY

23 TUESDAY

24 WEDNESDAY

25 THURSDAY

26 FRIDAY

27 SATURDAY   Passover Begins

28 SUNDAY

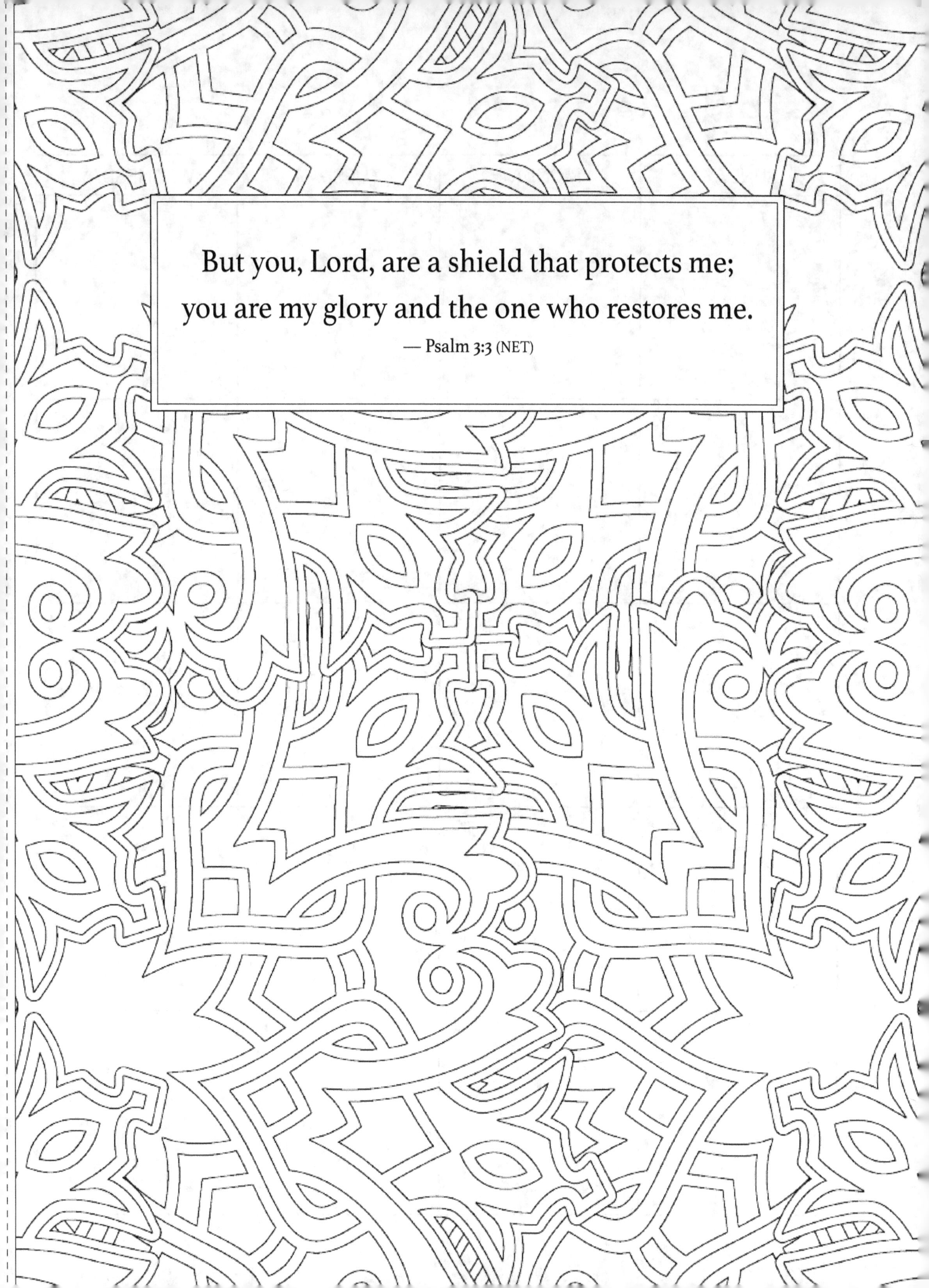
But you, Lord, are a shield that protects me;
you are my glory and the one who restores me.
— Psalm 3:3 (NET)

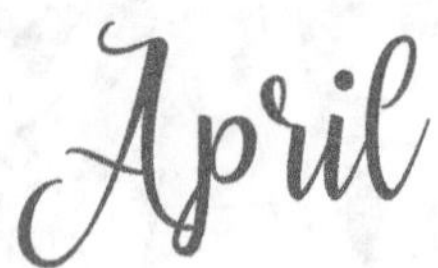

April

SUNDAY	MONDAY	TUESDAY	WEDNESDAY
4 Easter (Passover Ends)	5	6	7
11	12	13	14
18	19	20	21
25	26	27	28

April 2021

THURSDAY	FRIDAY	SATURDAY	NOTES
1	2 Good Friday	3	○
			○
			○
			○
			○
8	9	10	○
			○
			○
			○
			○
15 Tax Day	16	17	○
			○
			○
			○
22 Earth Day	23	24	○
			○
			○
			○
			○
29	30		NOTES

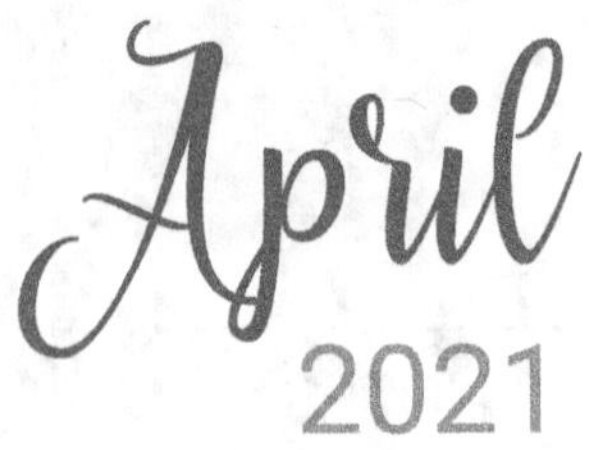

April
2021

29 MONDAY

30 TUESDAY

31 WEDNESDAY

01 THURSDAY

02 FRIDAY   Good Friday

03 SATURDAY

04 SUNDAY   Easter (Passover Ends)

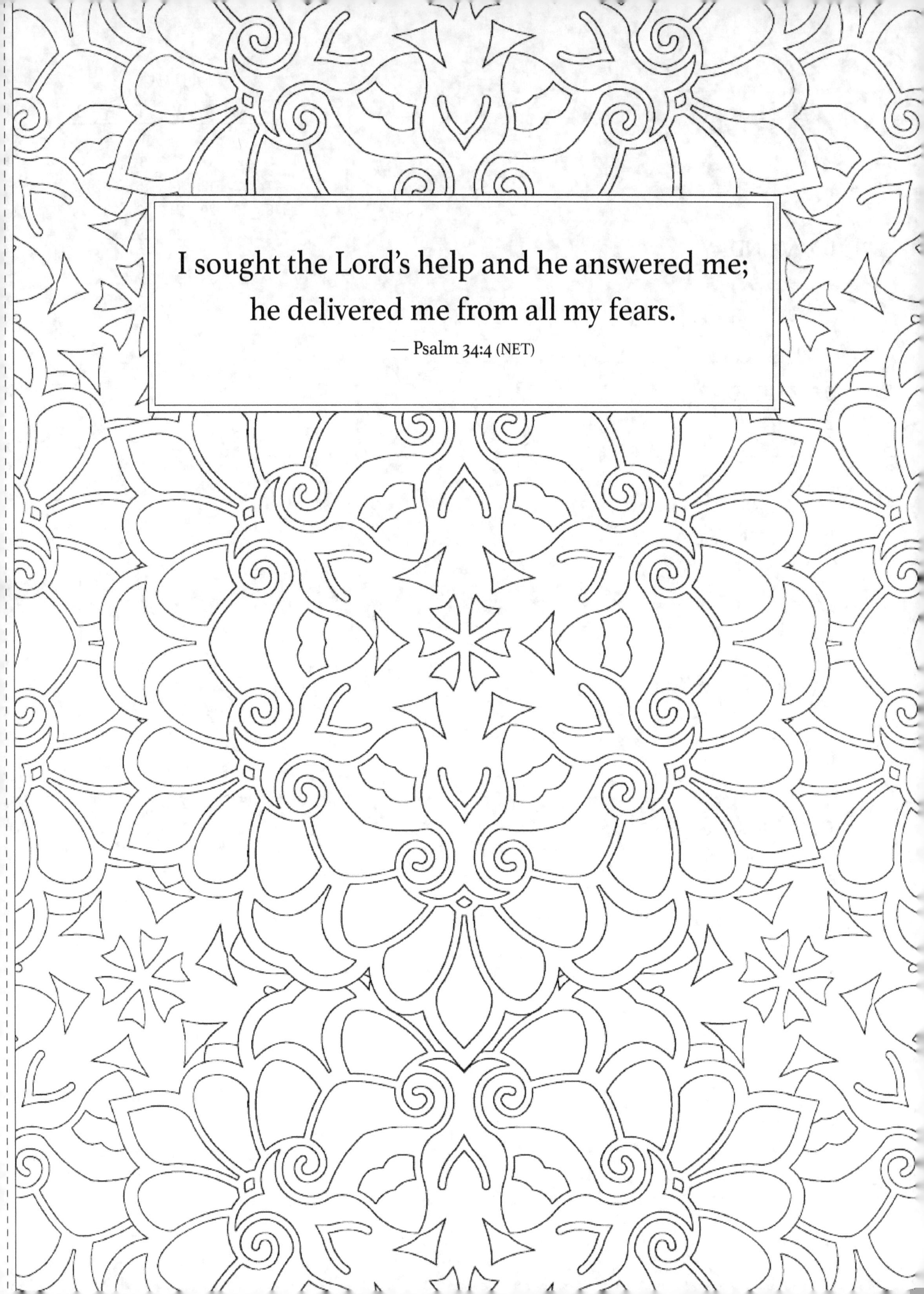

I sought the Lord's help and he answered me;
he delivered me from all my fears.
— Psalm 34:4 (NET)

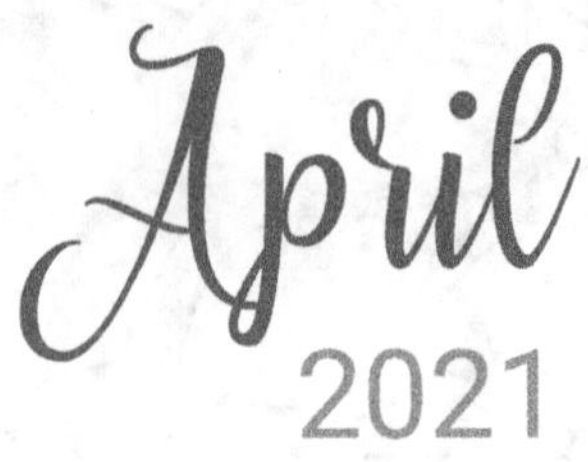

April
2021

05 MONDAY

06 TUESDAY

07 WEDNESDAY

08 THURSDAY

09 FRIDAY

10 SATURDAY

11 SUNDAY

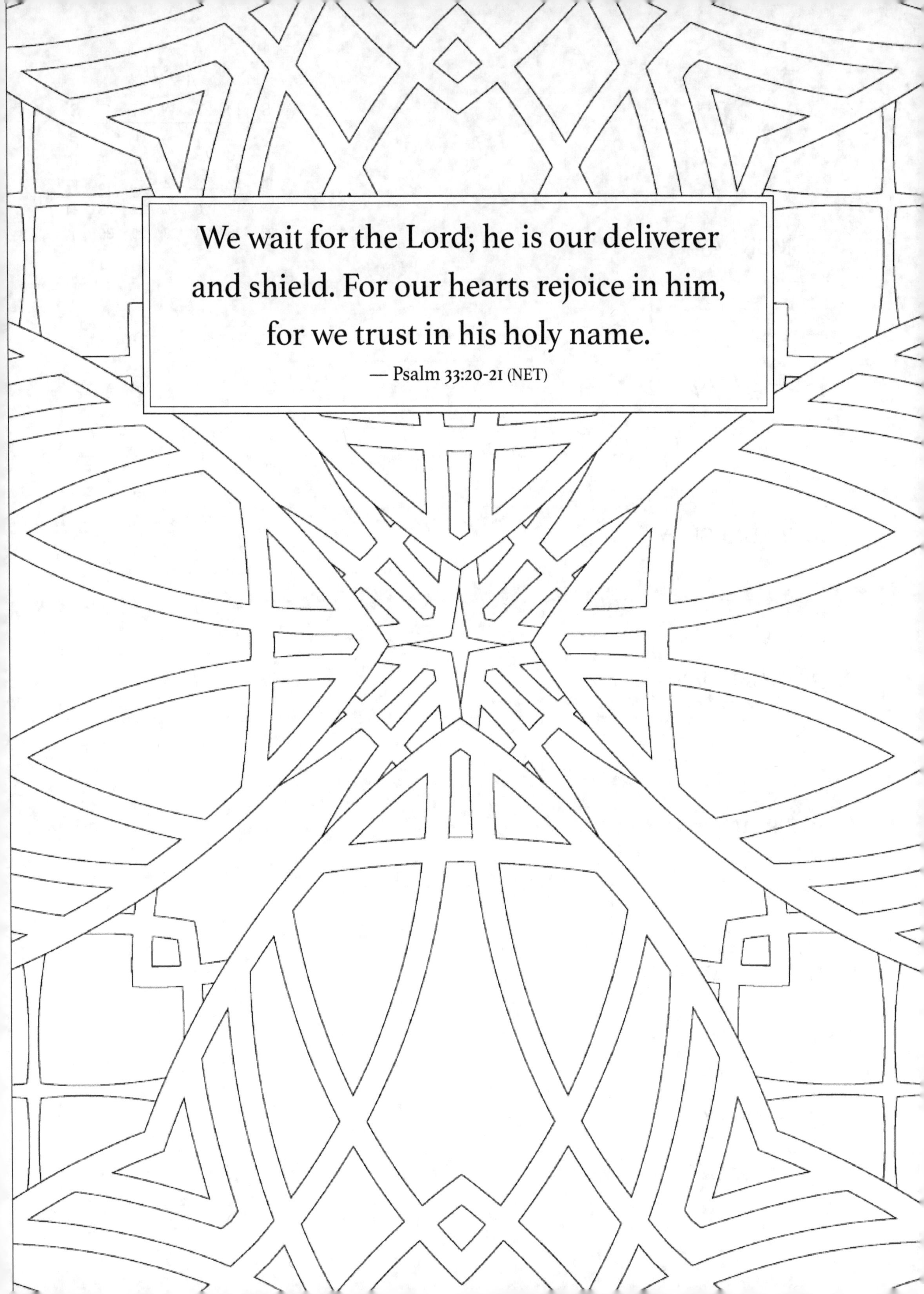

We wait for the Lord; he is our deliverer
and shield. For our hearts rejoice in him,
for we trust in his holy name.
— Psalm 33:20-21 (NET)

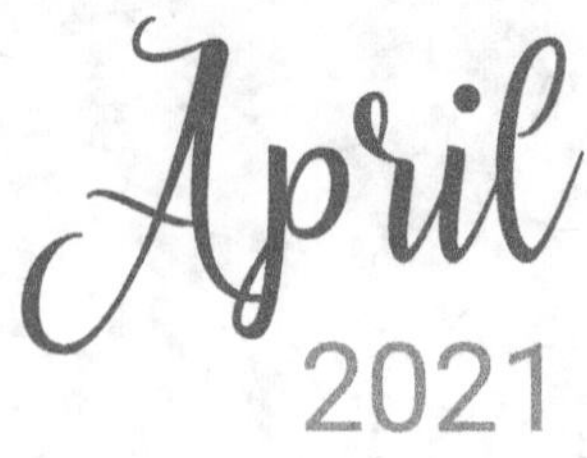

April
2021

12 MONDAY

13 TUESDAY

14 WEDNESDAY

15 THURSDAY Tax Day

16 FRIDAY

17 SATURDAY

18 SUNDAY

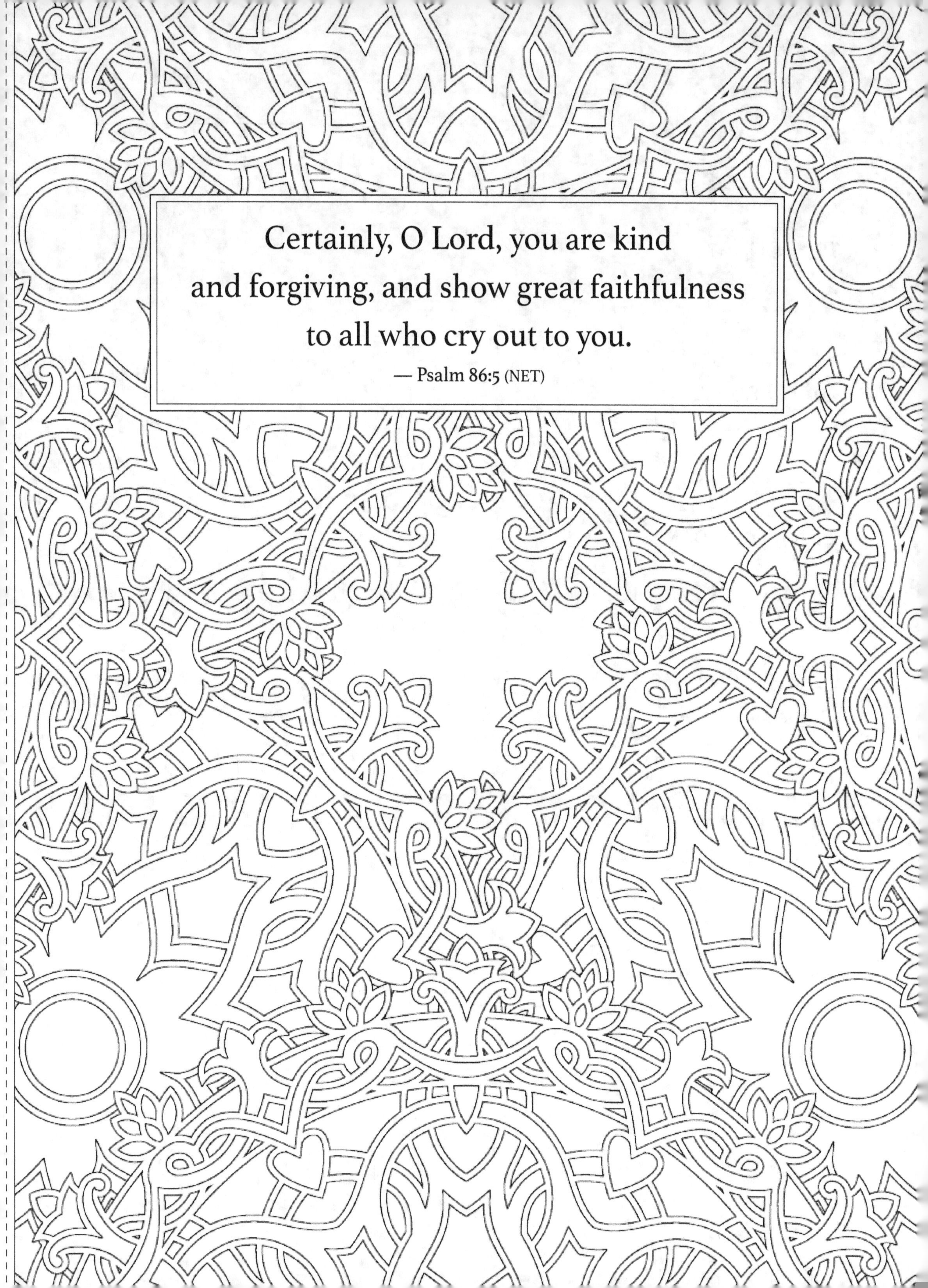

Certainly, O Lord, you are kind
and forgiving, and show great faithfulness
to all who cry out to you.
— Psalm 86:5 (NET)

April
2021

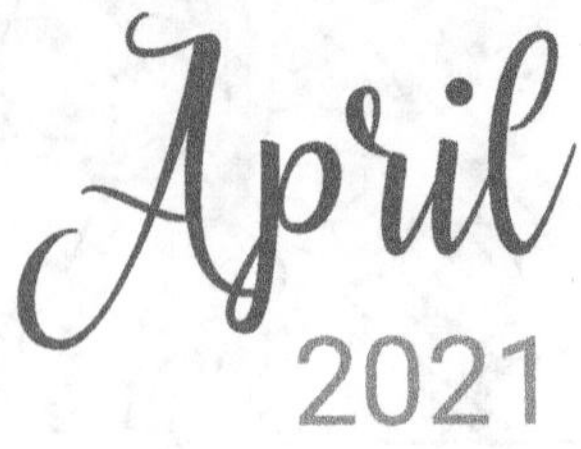

19 MONDAY

20 TUESDAY

21 WEDNESDAY

22 THURSDAY   Earth Day

23 FRIDAY

24 SATURDAY

25 SUNDAY

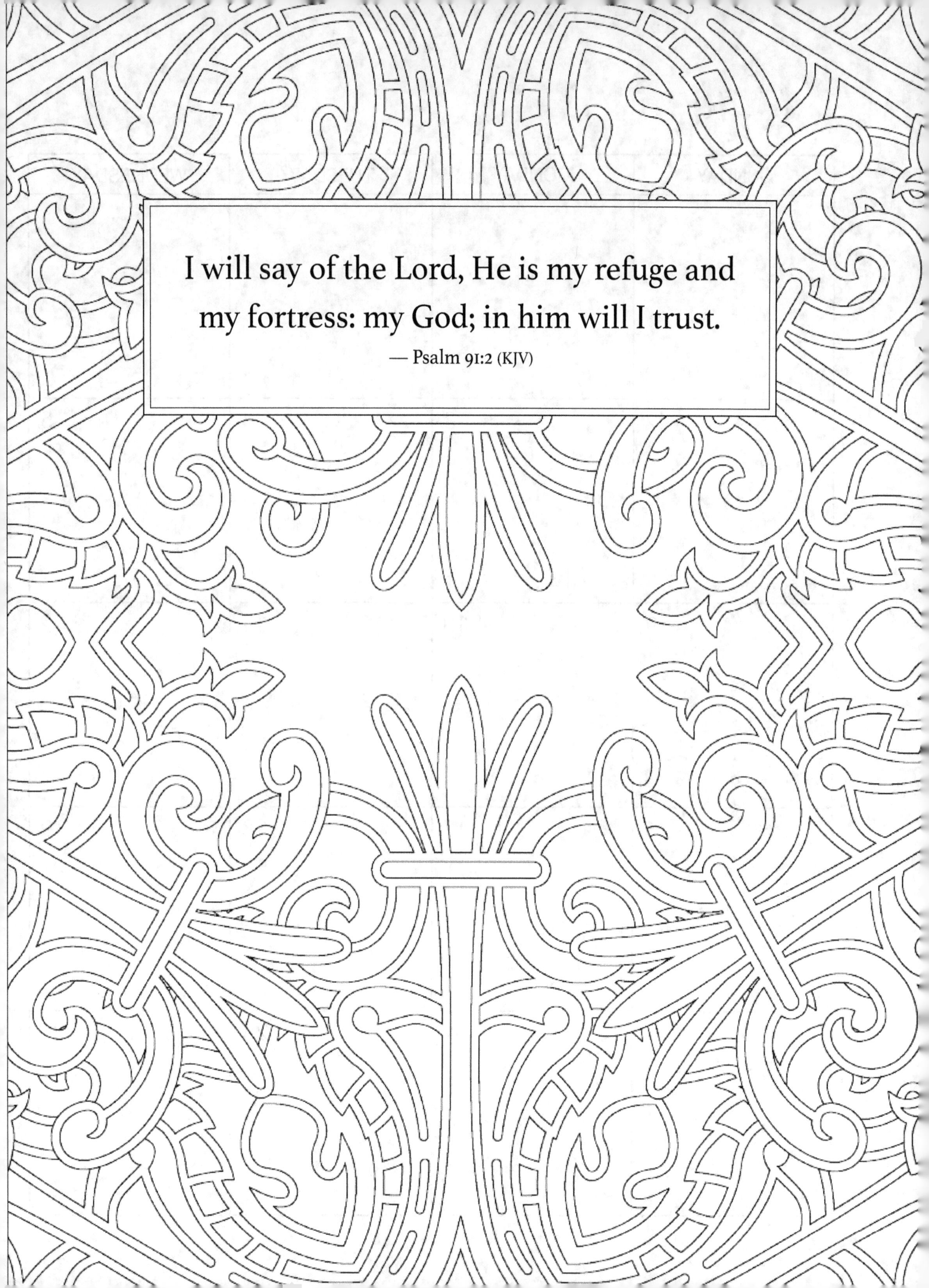
I will say of the Lord, He is my refuge and
my fortress: my God; in him will I trust.
— Psalm 91:2 (KJV)

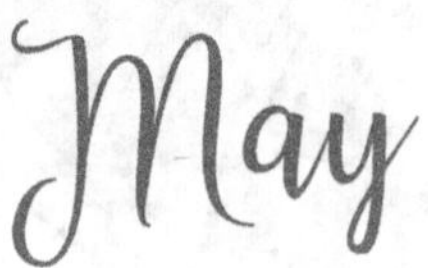

SUNDAY	MONDAY	TUESDAY	WEDNESDAY
2	3	4	5
9 Mother's Day	10	11	12
16	17	18	19
23 30	24 31 Memorial Day	25	26

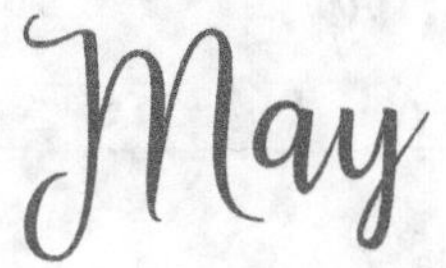 May 2021

THURSDAY	FRIDAY	SATURDAY	NOTES
		1	○
			○
			○
			○
			○
6	7	8	○
			○
			○
			○
13	14	15	○
			○
			○
			○
			○
20	21	22	○
			○
			○
			○
			○
27	28	29	NOTES

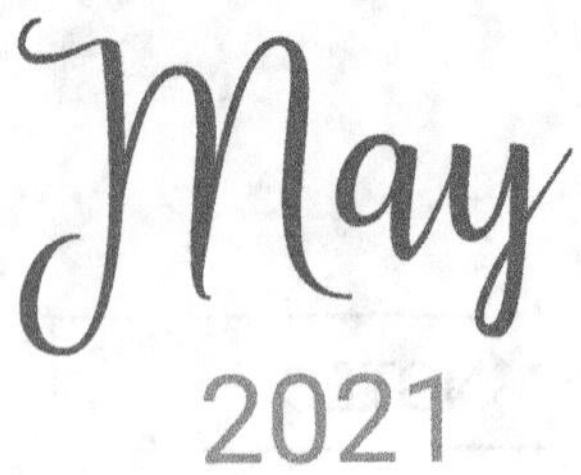

May
2021

26 MONDAY

27 TUESDAY

28 WEDNESDAY

29 THURSDAY

30 FRIDAY

01 SATURDAY

02 SUNDAY

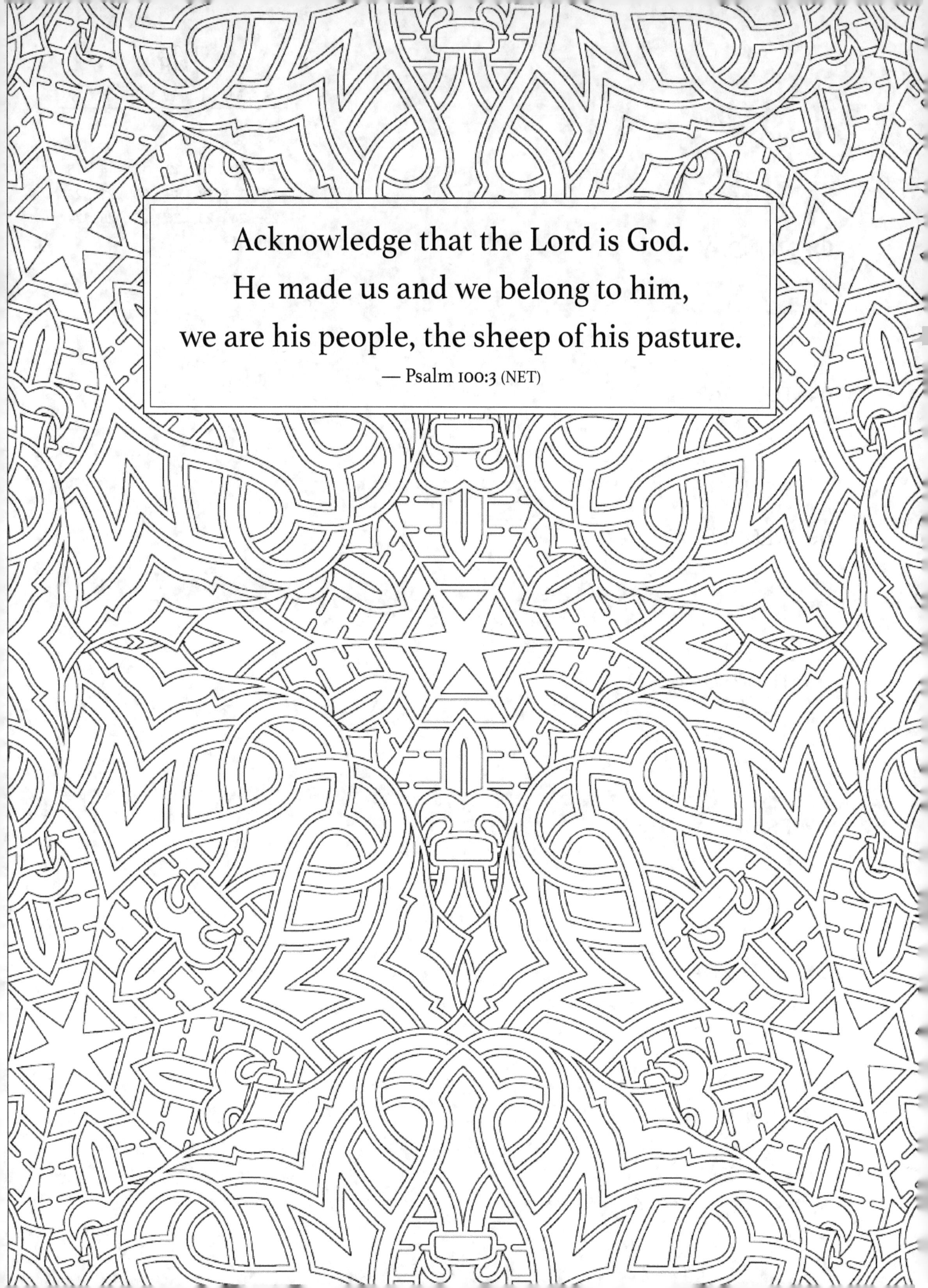

Acknowledge that the Lord is God.
He made us and we belong to him,
we are his people, the sheep of his pasture.
— Psalm 100:3 (NET)

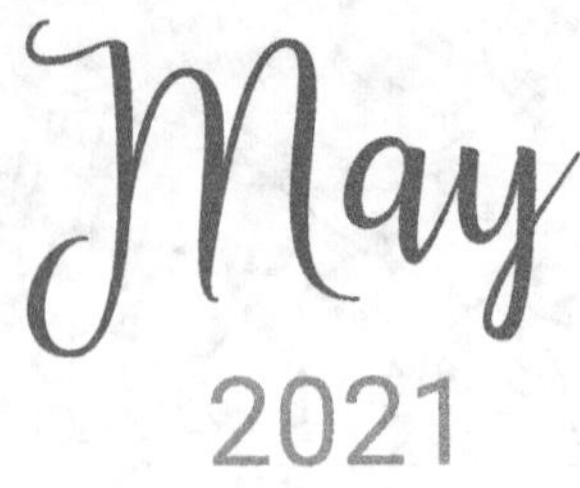

May
2021

03 MONDAY

04 TUESDAY

05 WEDNESDAY

06 THURSDAY

07 FRIDAY

08 SATURDAY

09 SUNDAY Mother's Day

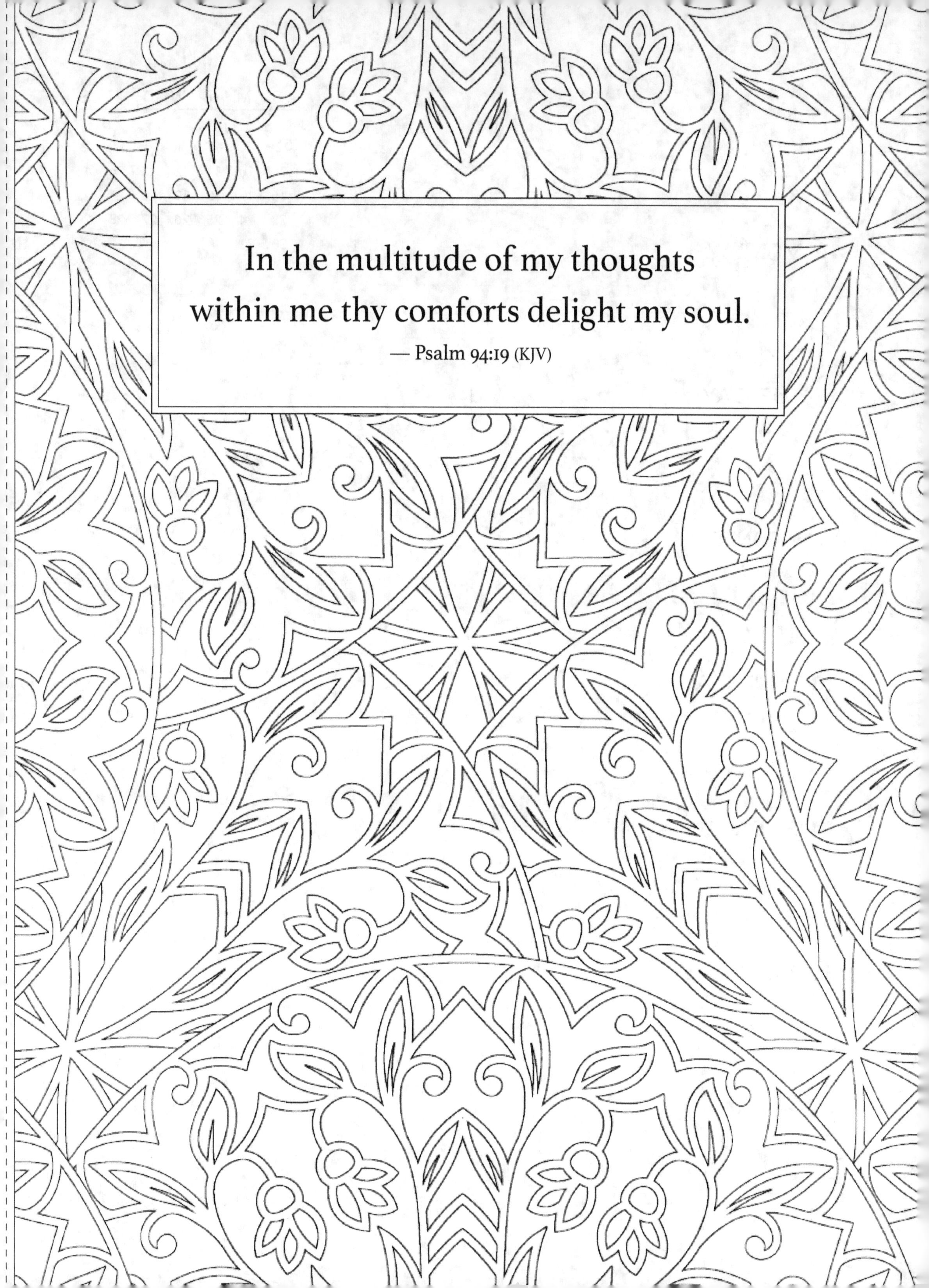

In the multitude of my thoughts
within me thy comforts delight my soul.
— Psalm 94:19 (KJV)

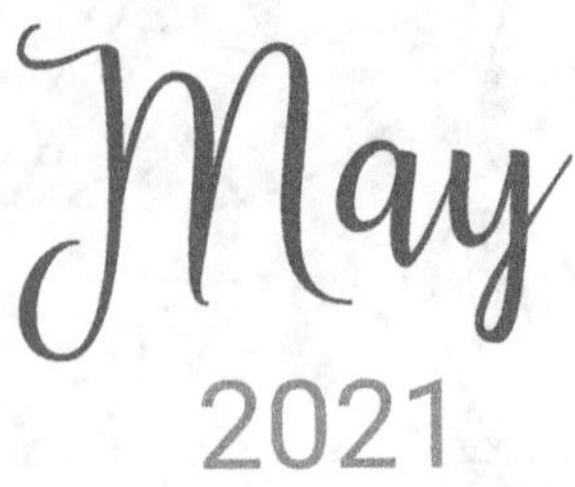

May
2021

10 MONDAY

11 TUESDAY

12 WEDNESDAY

13 THURSDAY

14 FRIDAY

15 SATURDAY

16 SUNDAY

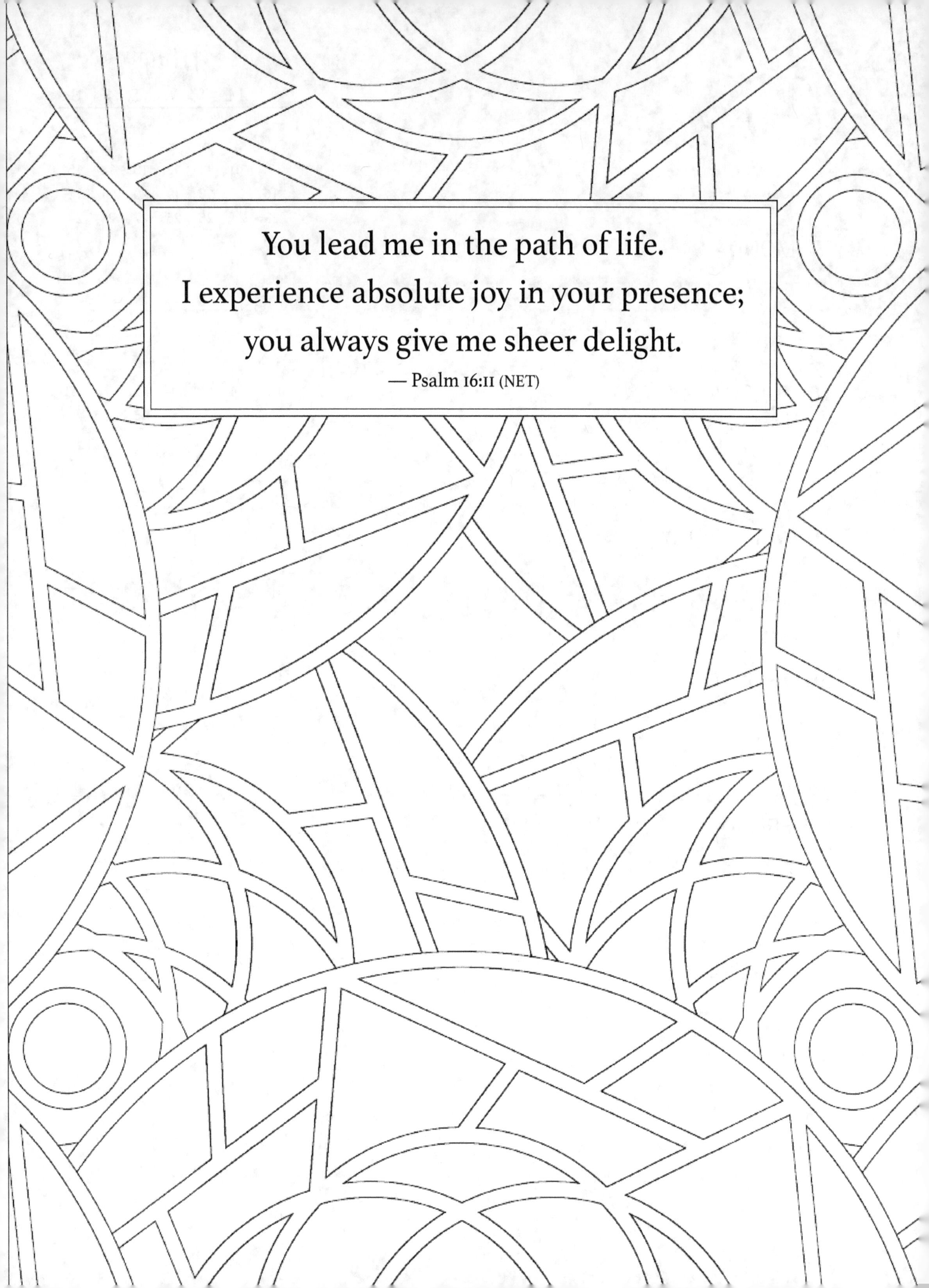

You lead me in the path of life.
I experience absolute joy in your presence;
you always give me sheer delight.
— Psalm 16:11 (NET)

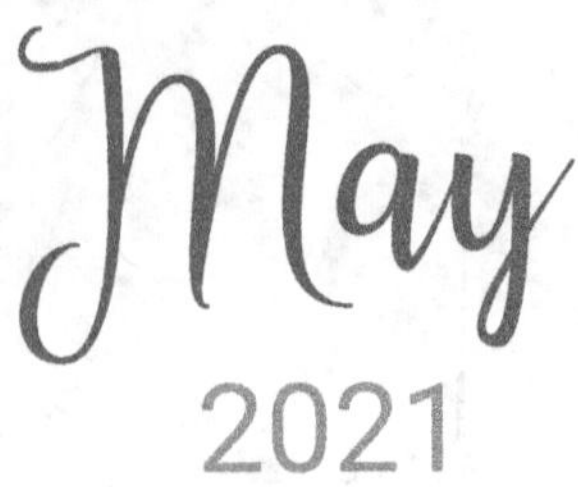

May

2021

17 MONDAY

18 TUESDAY

19 WEDNESDAY

20 THURSDAY

21 FRIDAY

22 SATURDAY

23 SUNDAY

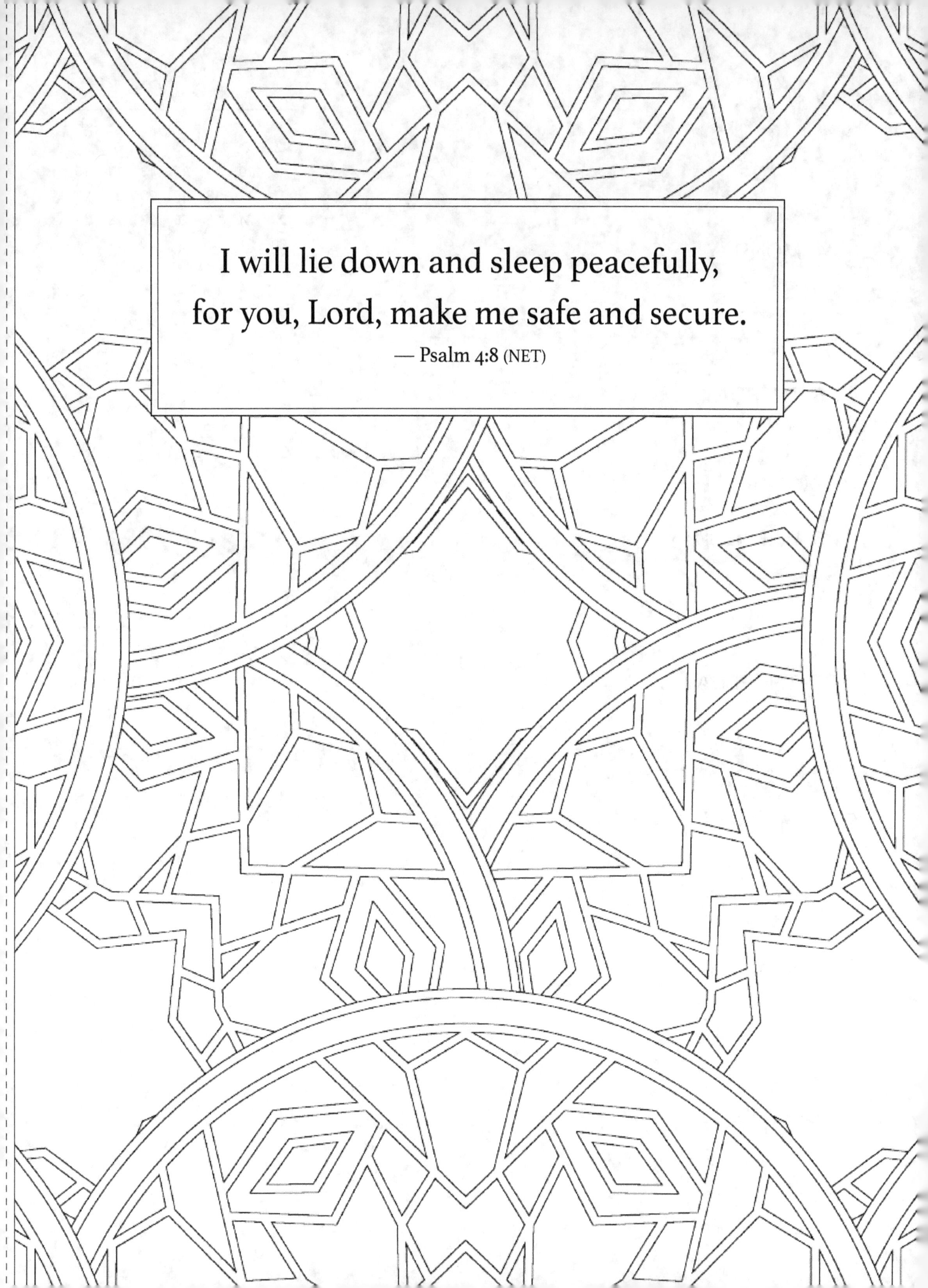
I will lie down and sleep peacefully,
for you, Lord, make me safe and secure.
— Psalm 4:8 (NET)

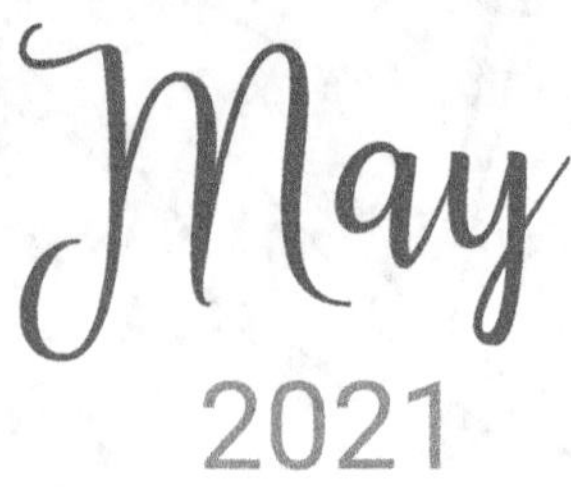

24 MONDAY

25 TUESDAY

26 WEDNESDAY

27 THURSDAY

28 FRIDAY

29 SATURDAY

30 SUNDAY

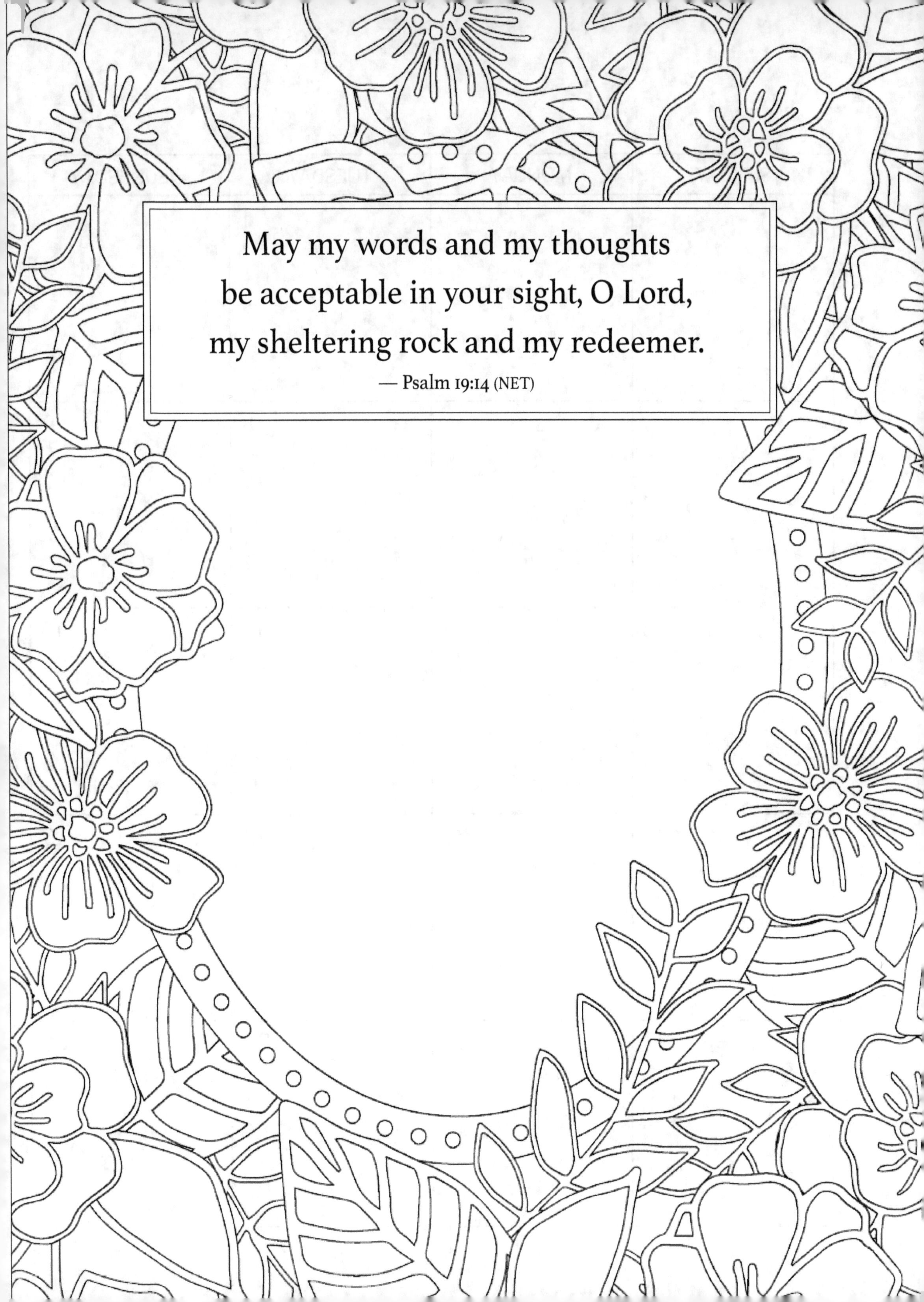
May my words and my thoughts
be acceptable in your sight, O Lord,
my sheltering rock and my redeemer.
— Psalm 19:14 (NET)

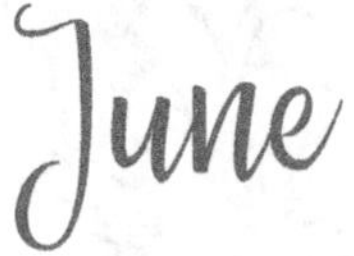

June 2021

SUNDAY	MONDAY	TUESDAY	WEDNESDAY
		1	2
6	7	8	9
13	14 Flag Day	15	16
20 Father's Day	21 First Day of Summer	22	23
27	28	29	30

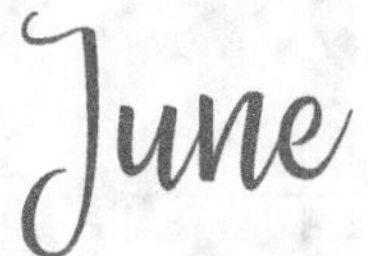

June

2021

THURSDAY	FRIDAY	SATURDAY	NOTES
3	4	5	○
			○
			○
			○
			○
10	11	12	○
			○
			○
			○
			○
17	18	19	○
			○
			○
			○
			○
24	25	26	○
			○
			○
			○
			○
			NOTES

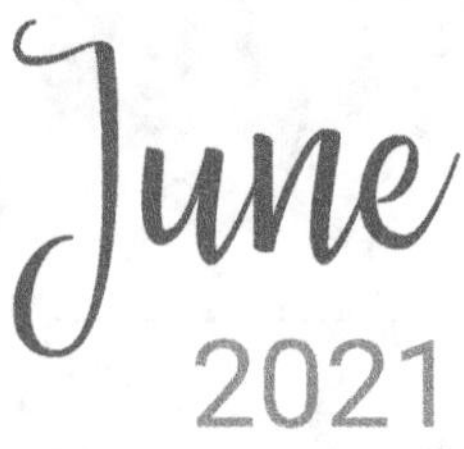

June
2021

31 MONDAY Memorial Day

01 TUESDAY

02 WEDNESDAY

03 THURSDAY

04 FRIDAY

05 SATURDAY

06 SUNDAY

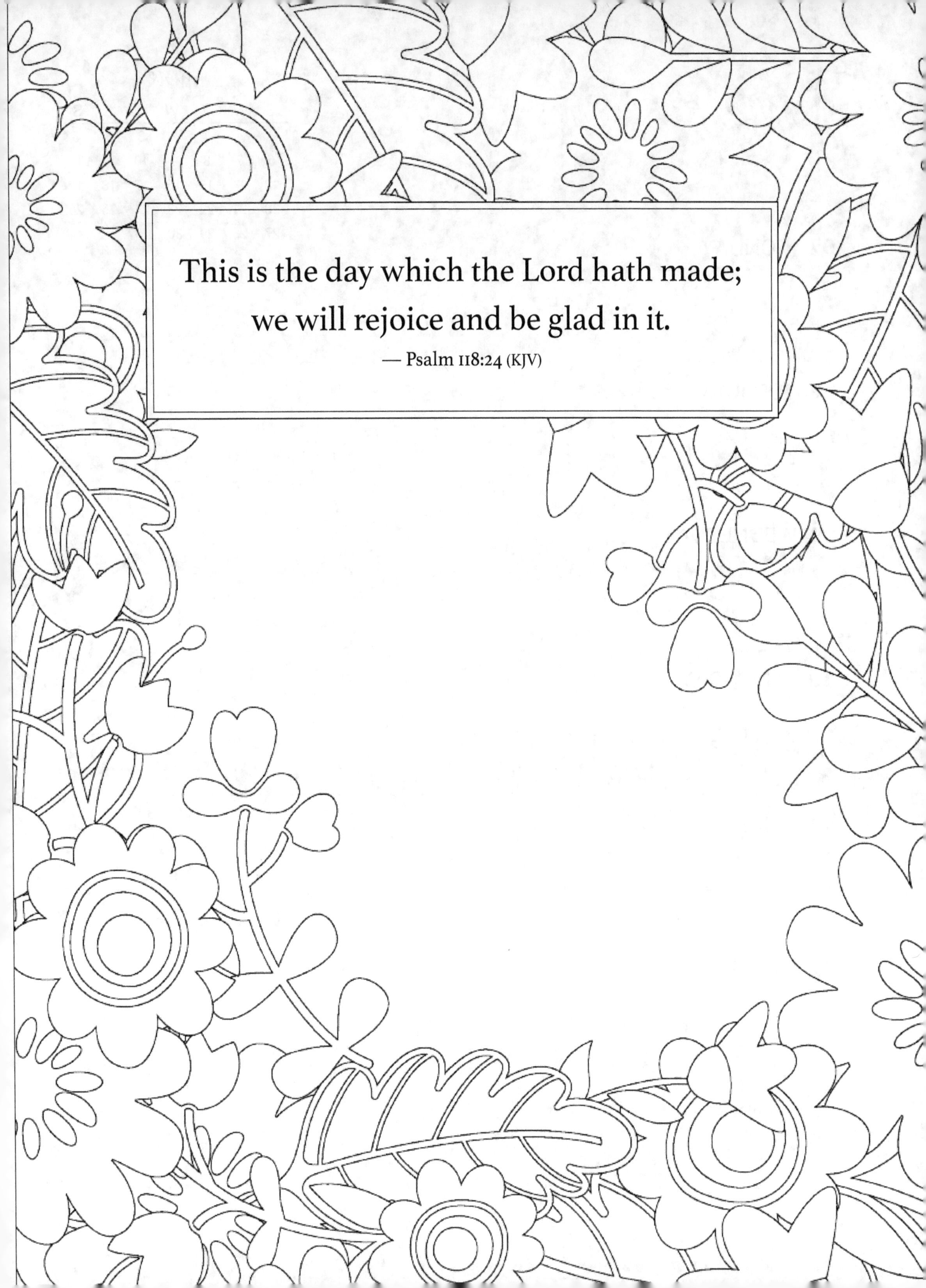

This is the day which the Lord hath made;
we will rejoice and be glad in it.
— Psalm 118:24 (KJV)

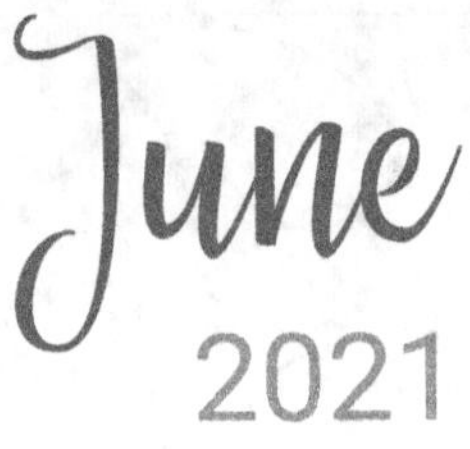

June
2021

07 MONDAY

08 TUESDAY

09 WEDNESDAY

10 THURSDAY

11 FRIDAY

12 SATURDAY

13 SUNDAY

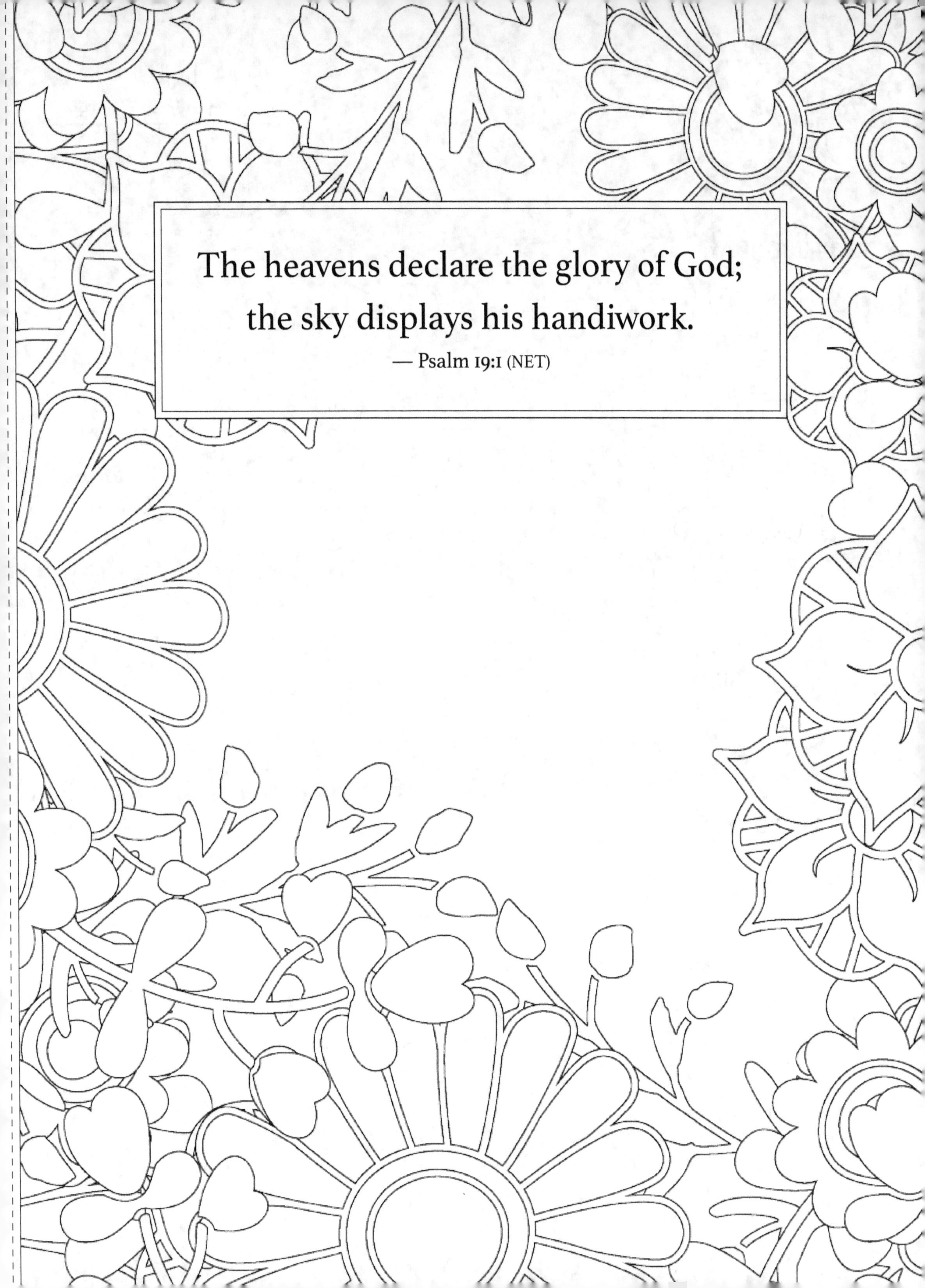

The heavens declare the glory of God;
the sky displays his handiwork.

— Psalm 19:1 (NET)

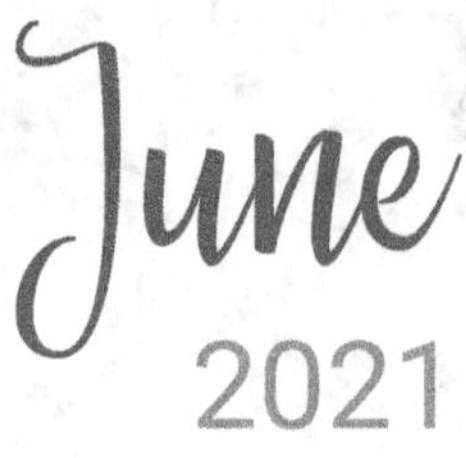

June
2021

14 MONDAY   Flag Day

15 TUESDAY

16 WEDNESDAY

17 THURSDAY

18 FRIDAY

19 SATURDAY

20 SUNDAY   Father's Day

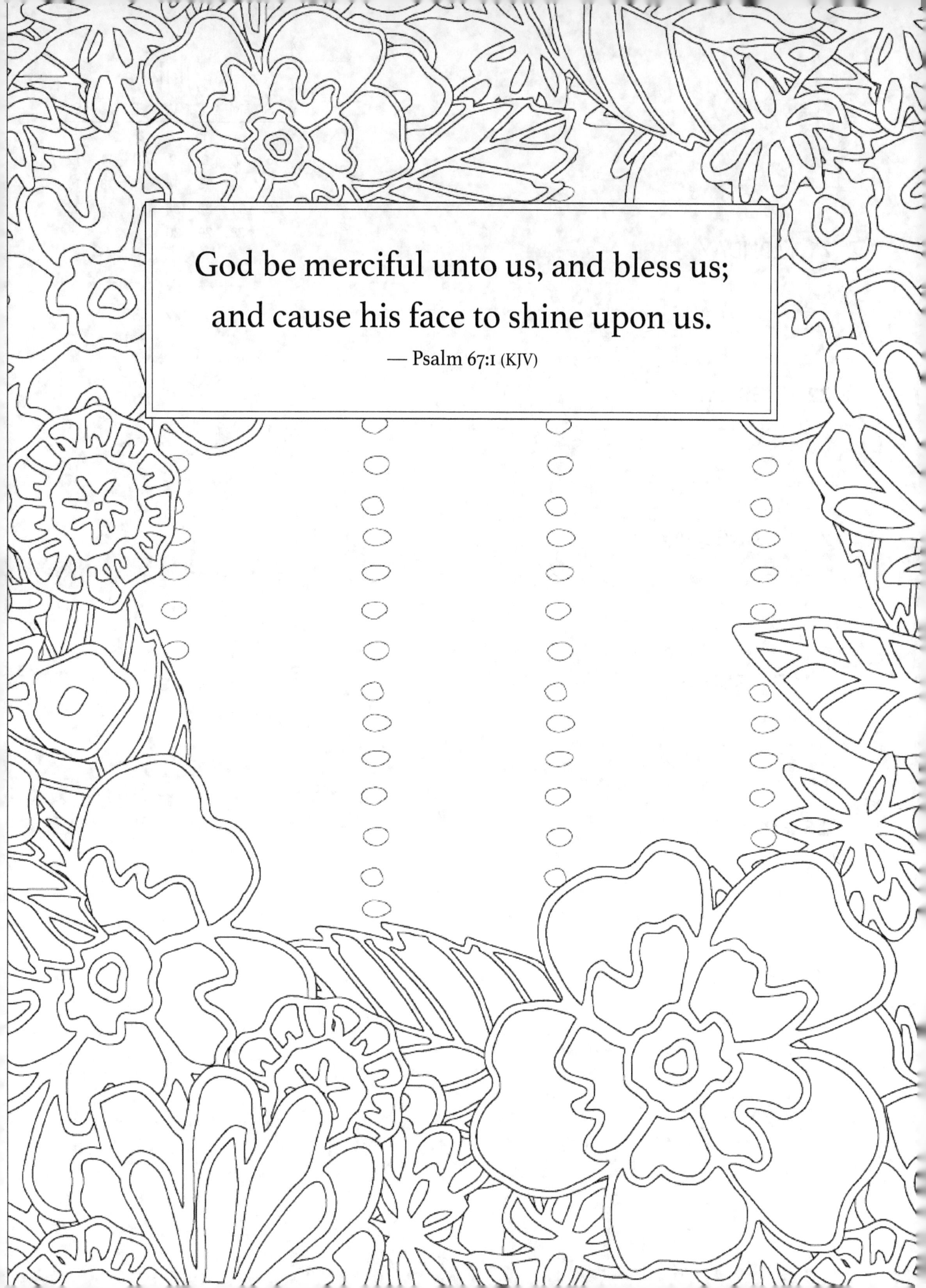

God be merciful unto us, and bless us;
and cause his face to shine upon us.
— Psalm 67:1 (KJV)

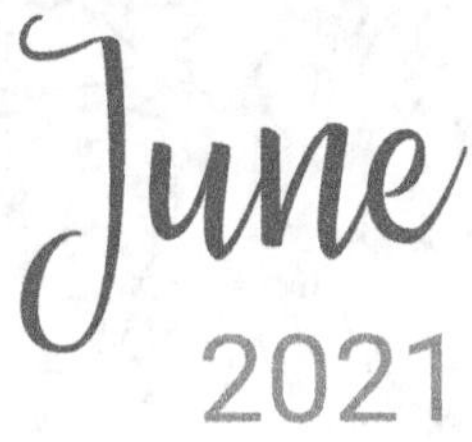

June
2021

21 MONDAY First Day of Summer

22 TUESDAY

23 WEDNESDAY

24 THURSDAY

25 FRIDAY

26 SATURDAY

27 SUNDAY

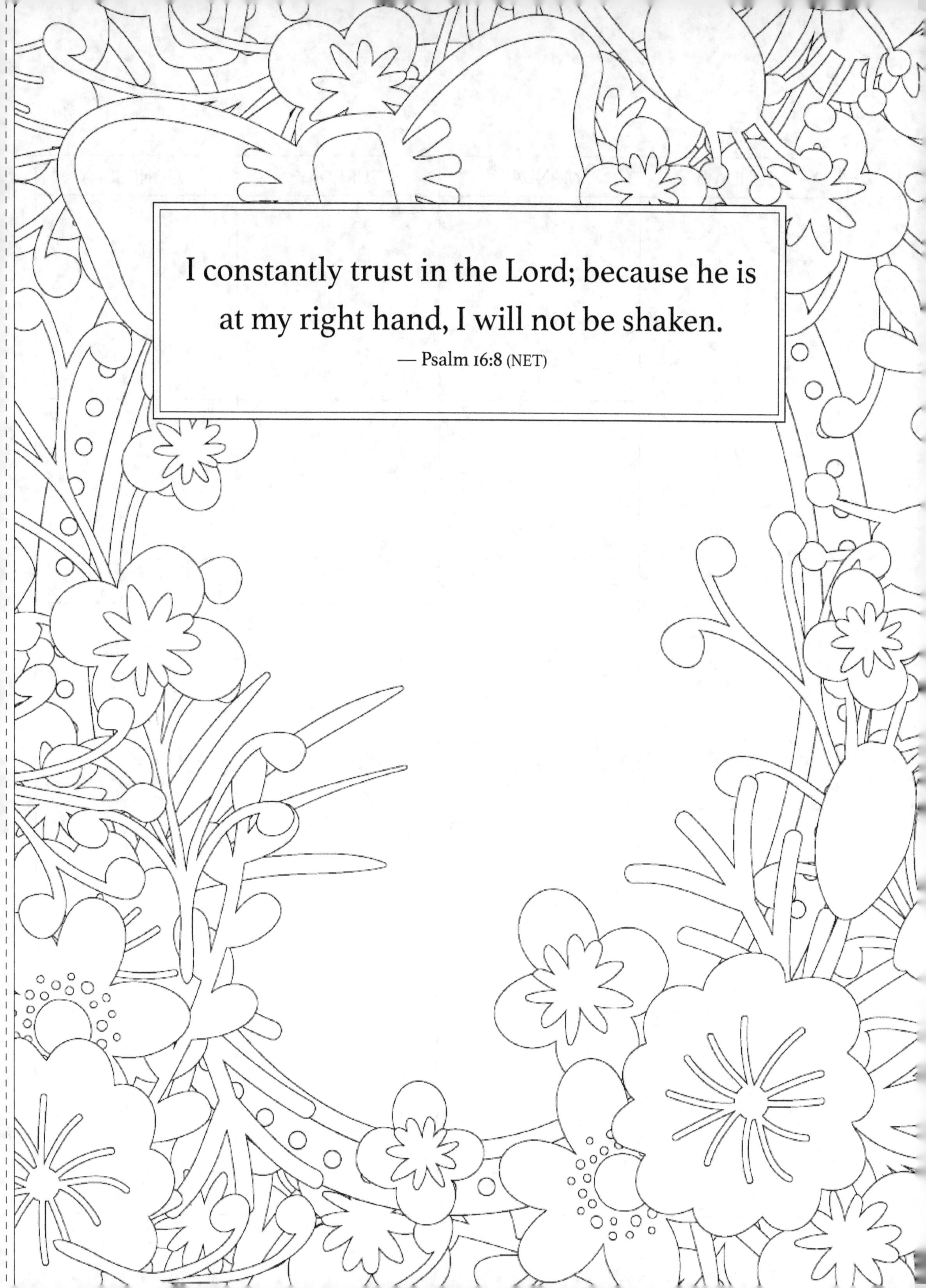

I constantly trust in the Lord; because he is
at my right hand, I will not be shaken.
— Psalm 16:8 (NET)

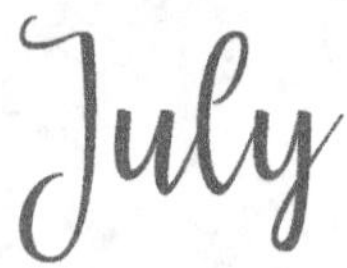

July 2021

SUNDAY	MONDAY	TUESDAY	WEDNESDAY
4 Independence Day	5	6	7
11	12	13	14
18	19	20	21
25	26	27	28

THURSDAY	FRIDAY	SATURDAY	NOTES
1	2	3	○
			○
			○
			○
			○
8	9	10	○
			○
			○
			○
15	16	17	○
			○
			○
			○
			○
22	23	24	○
			○
			○
			○
			○
29	30		NOTES

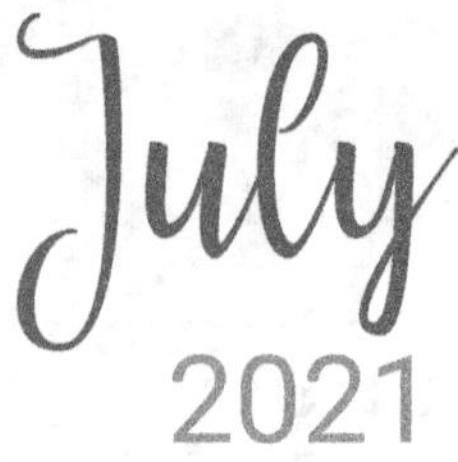

July
2021

28 MONDAY

29 TUESDAY

30 WEDNESDAY

01 THURSDAY

02 FRIDAY

03 SATURDAY

04 SUNDAY   Independence Day

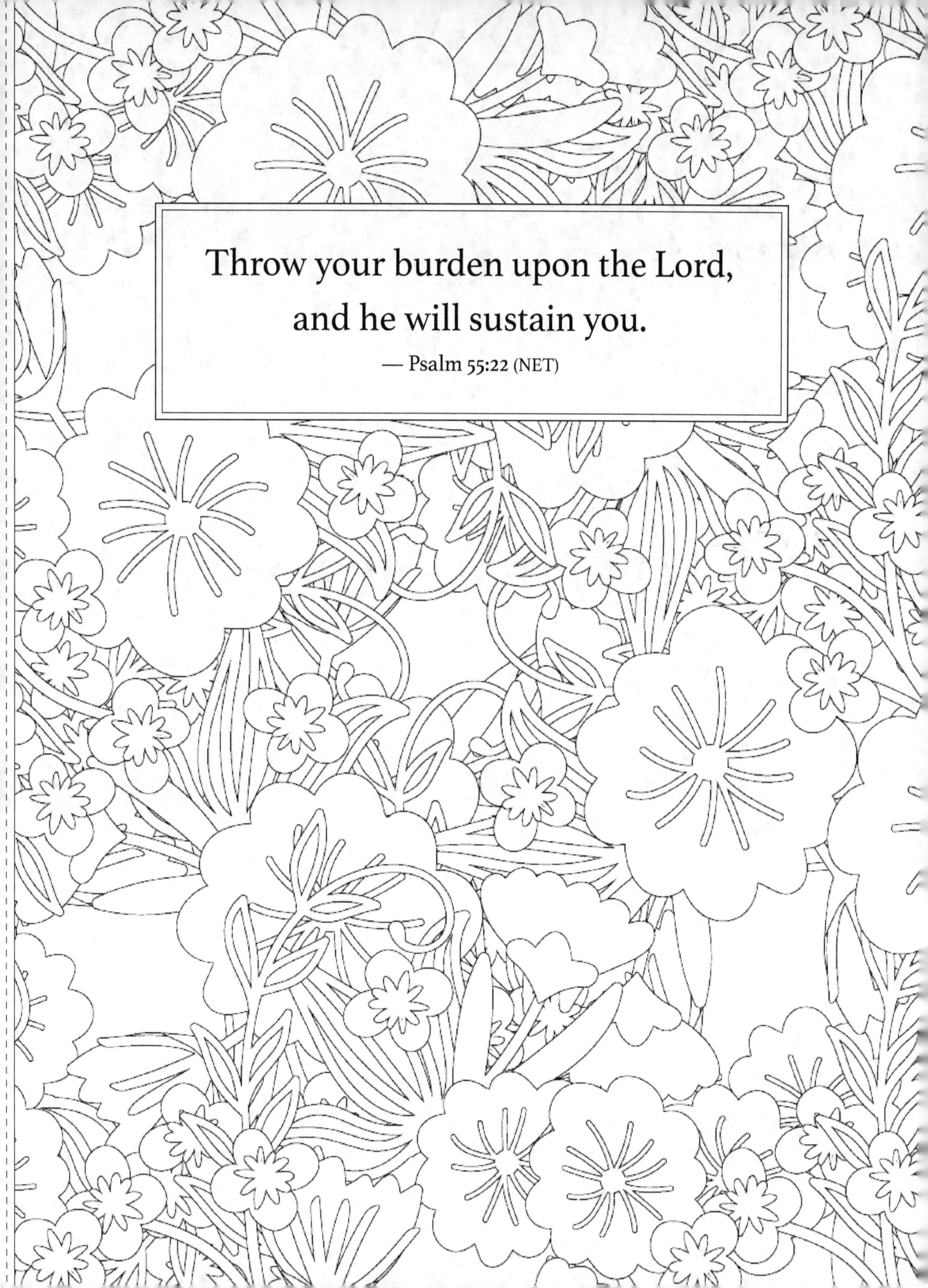

Throw your burden upon the Lord,
and he will sustain you.
— Psalm 55:22 (NET)

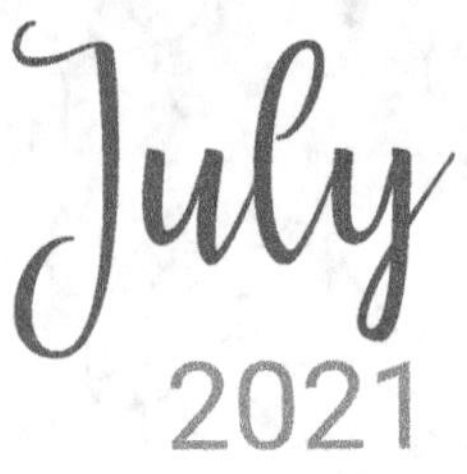

July
2021

05 MONDAY

06 TUESDAY

07 WEDNESDAY

08 THURSDAY

09 FRIDAY

10 SATURDAY

11 SUNDAY

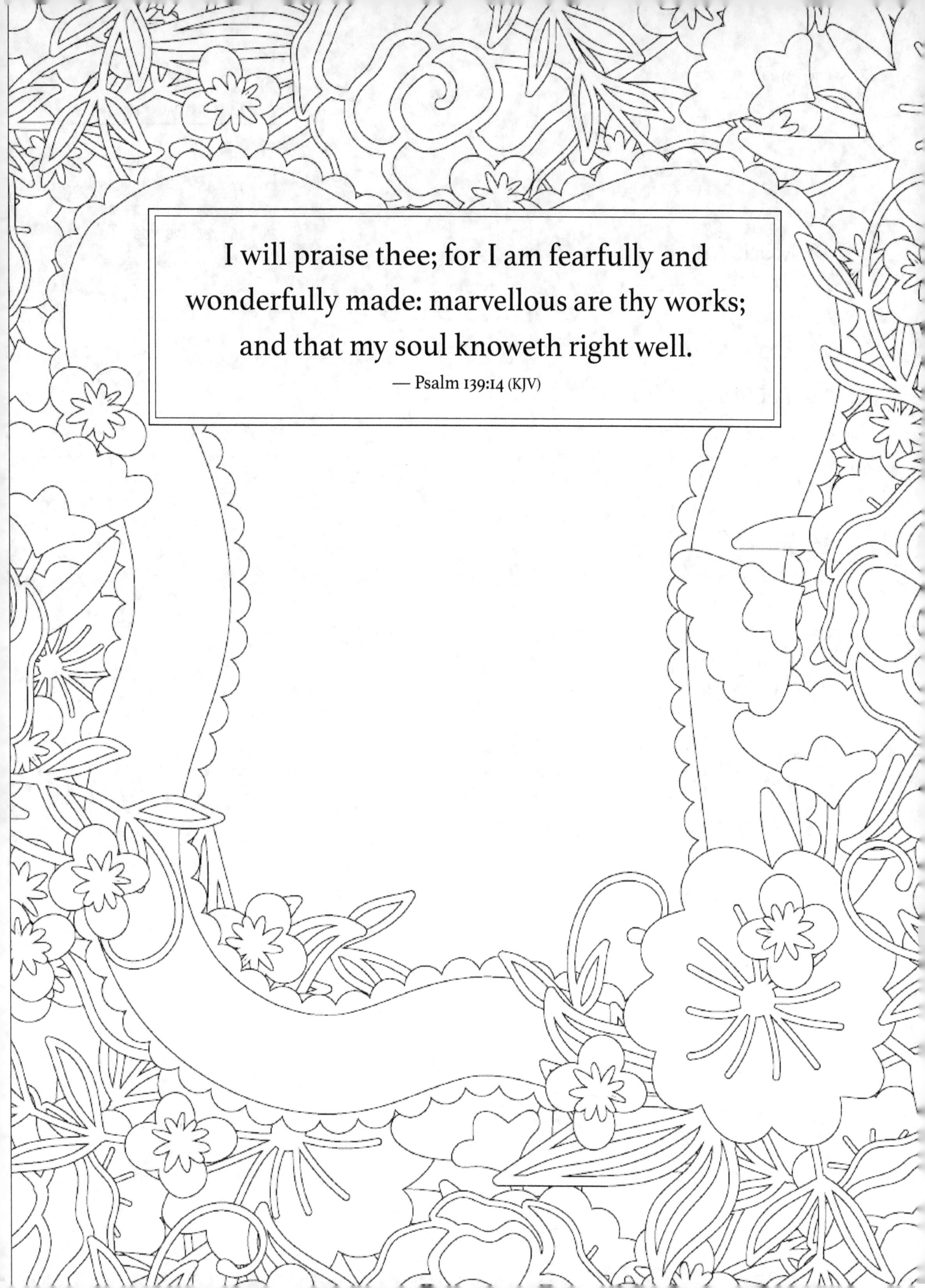

I will praise thee; for I am fearfully and wonderfully made: marvellous are thy works; and that my soul knoweth right well.
— Psalm 139:14 (KJV)

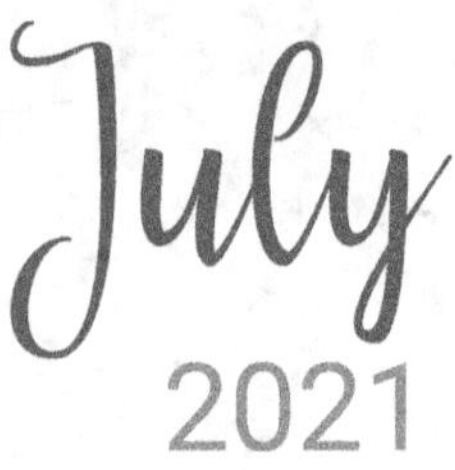

July
2021

12 MONDAY

13 TUESDAY

14 WEDNESDAY

15 THURSDAY

16 FRIDAY

17 SATURDAY

18 SUNDAY

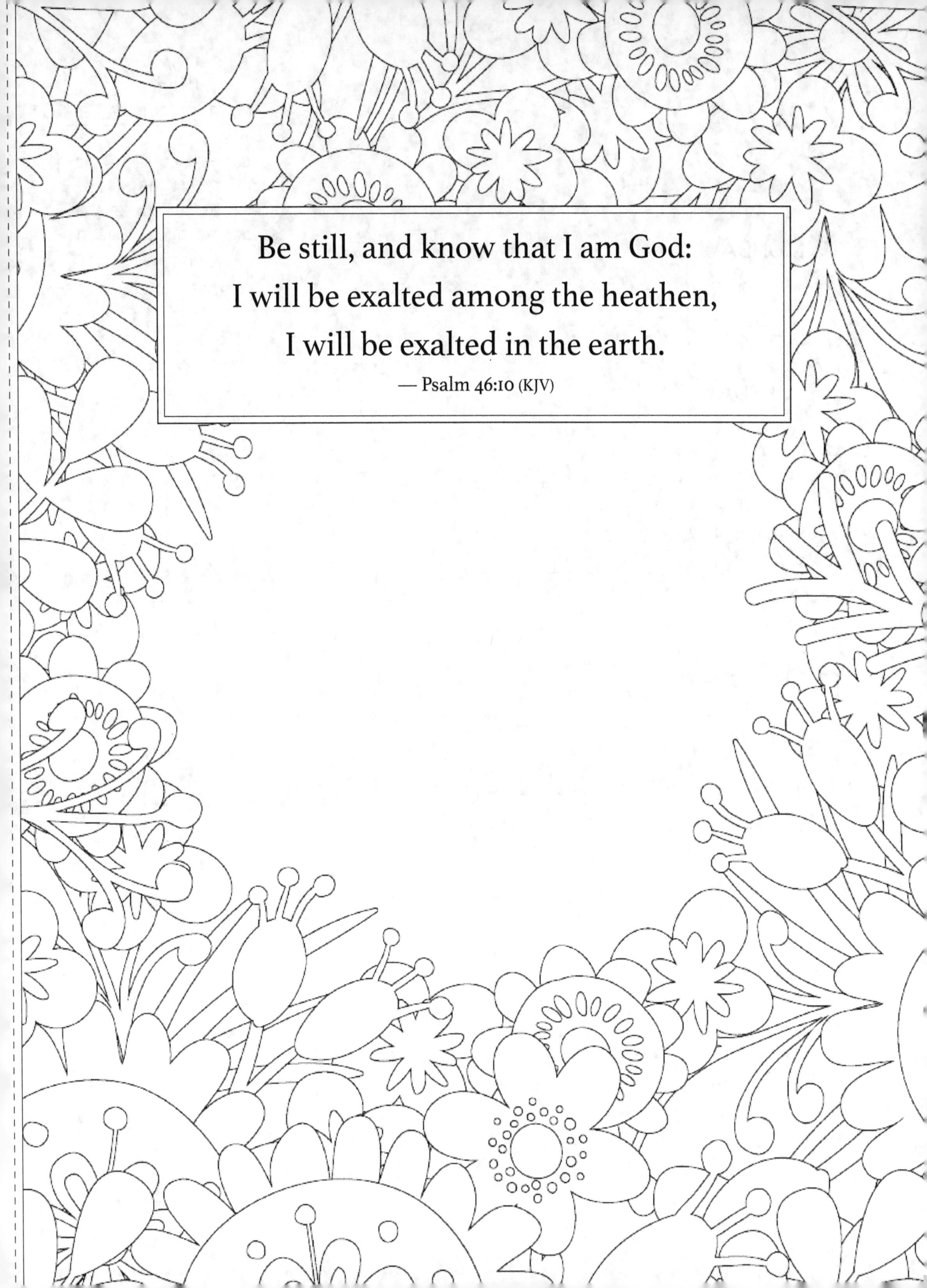

Be still, and know that I am God:
I will be exalted among the heathen,
I will be exalted in the earth.
— Psalm 46:10 (KJV)

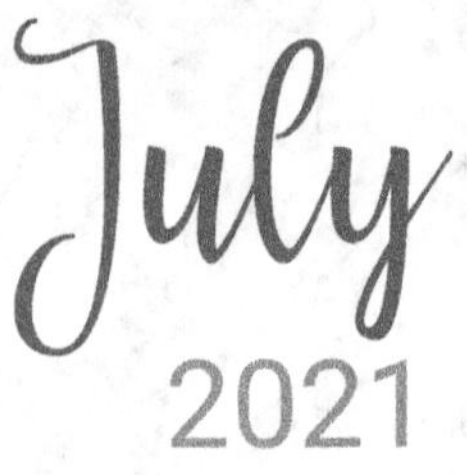

July
2021

19 MONDAY

20 TUESDAY

21 WEDNESDAY

22 THURSDAY

23 FRIDAY

24 SATURDAY

25 SUNDAY

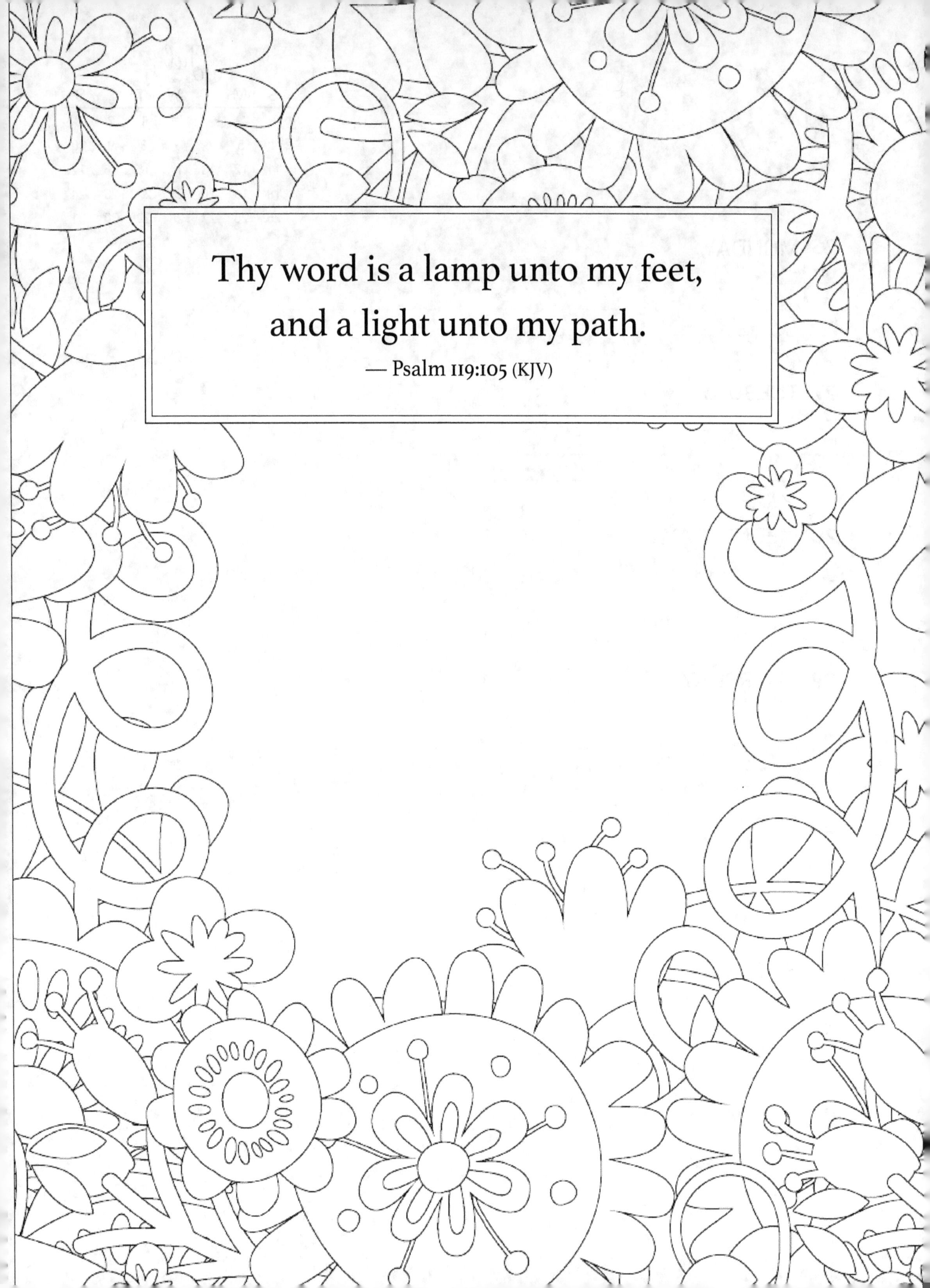

Thy word is a lamp unto my feet,
and a light unto my path.
— Psalm 119:105 (KJV)

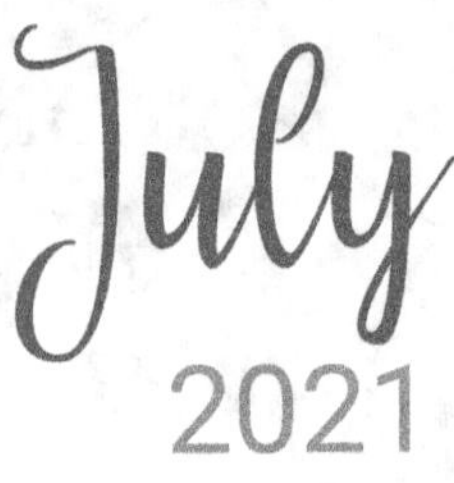

July
2021

26 MONDAY

27 TUESDAY

28 WEDNESDAY

29 THURSDAY

30 FRIDAY

31 SATURDAY

01 SUNDAY

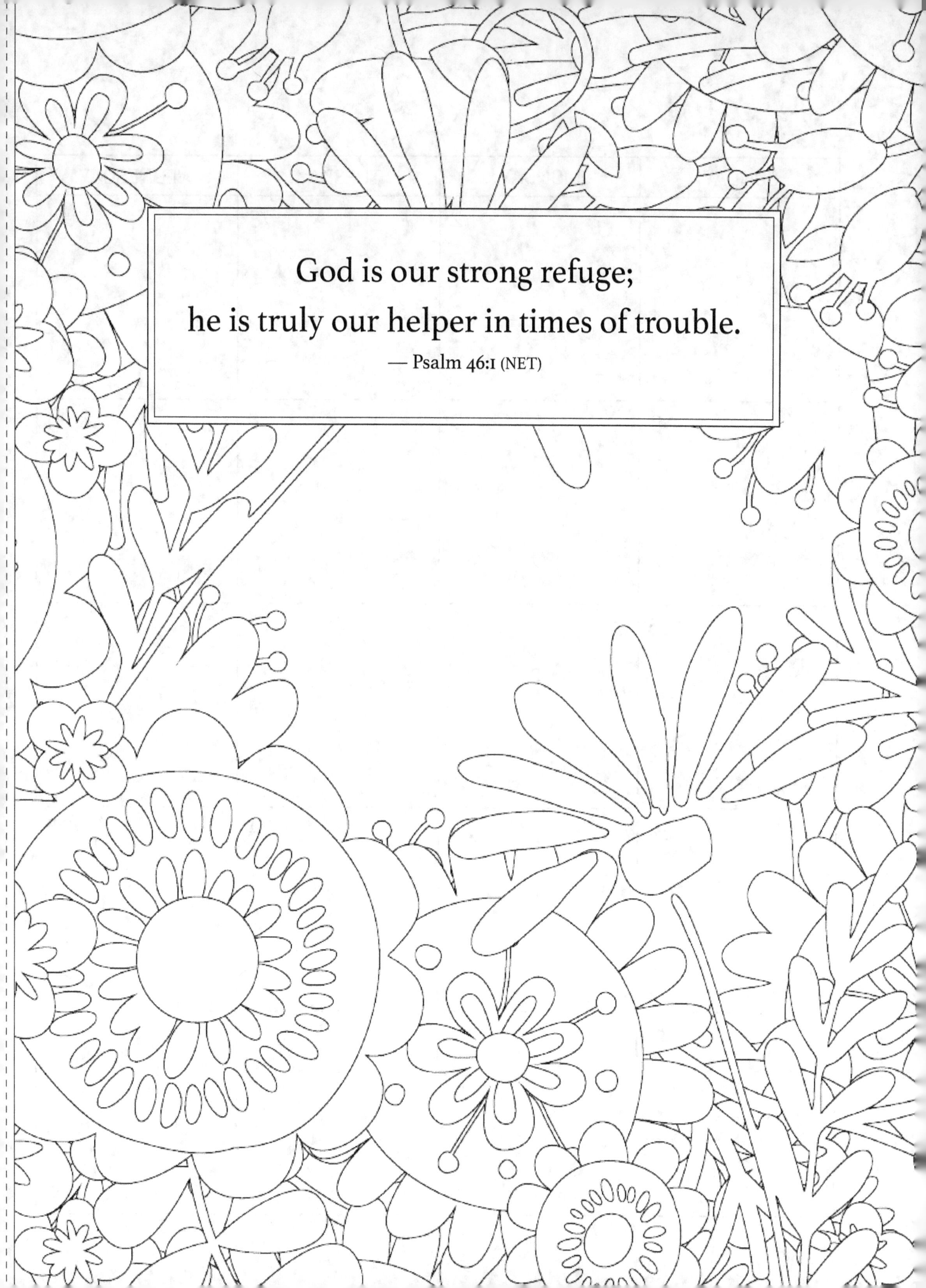

God is our strong refuge;
he is truly our helper in times of trouble.
— Psalm 46:1 (NET)

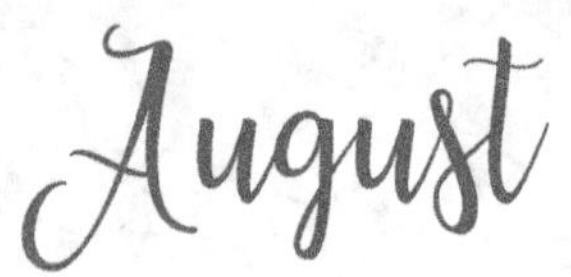

August 2021

SUNDAY	MONDAY	TUESDAY	WEDNESDAY
1	2	3	4
8	9	10	11
15	16	17	18
22	23	24	25
29	30	31	

August 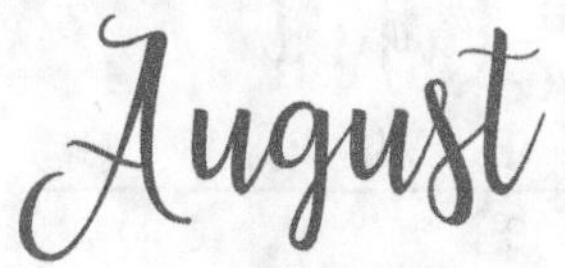 2021

THURSDAY	FRIDAY	SATURDAY	NOTES
5	6	7	○
			○
			○
			○
			○
12	13	14	○
			○
			○
			○
			○
19	20	21	○
			○
			○
			○
			○
26	27	28	○
			○
			○
			○
			○
			NOTES

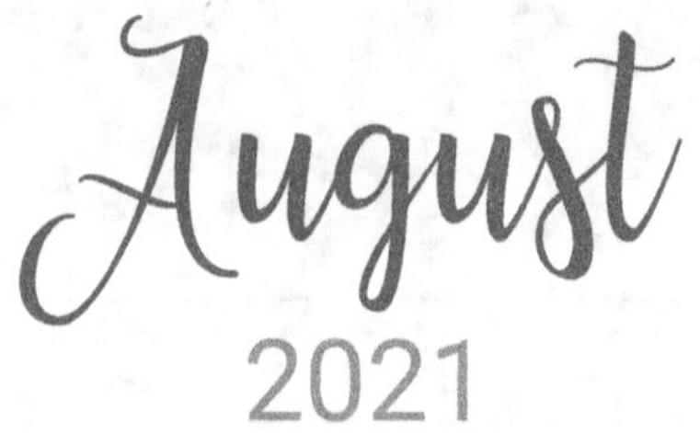

August
2021

02 MONDAY

03 TUESDAY

04 WEDNESDAY

05 THURSDAY

06 FRIDAY

07 SATURDAY

08 SUNDAY

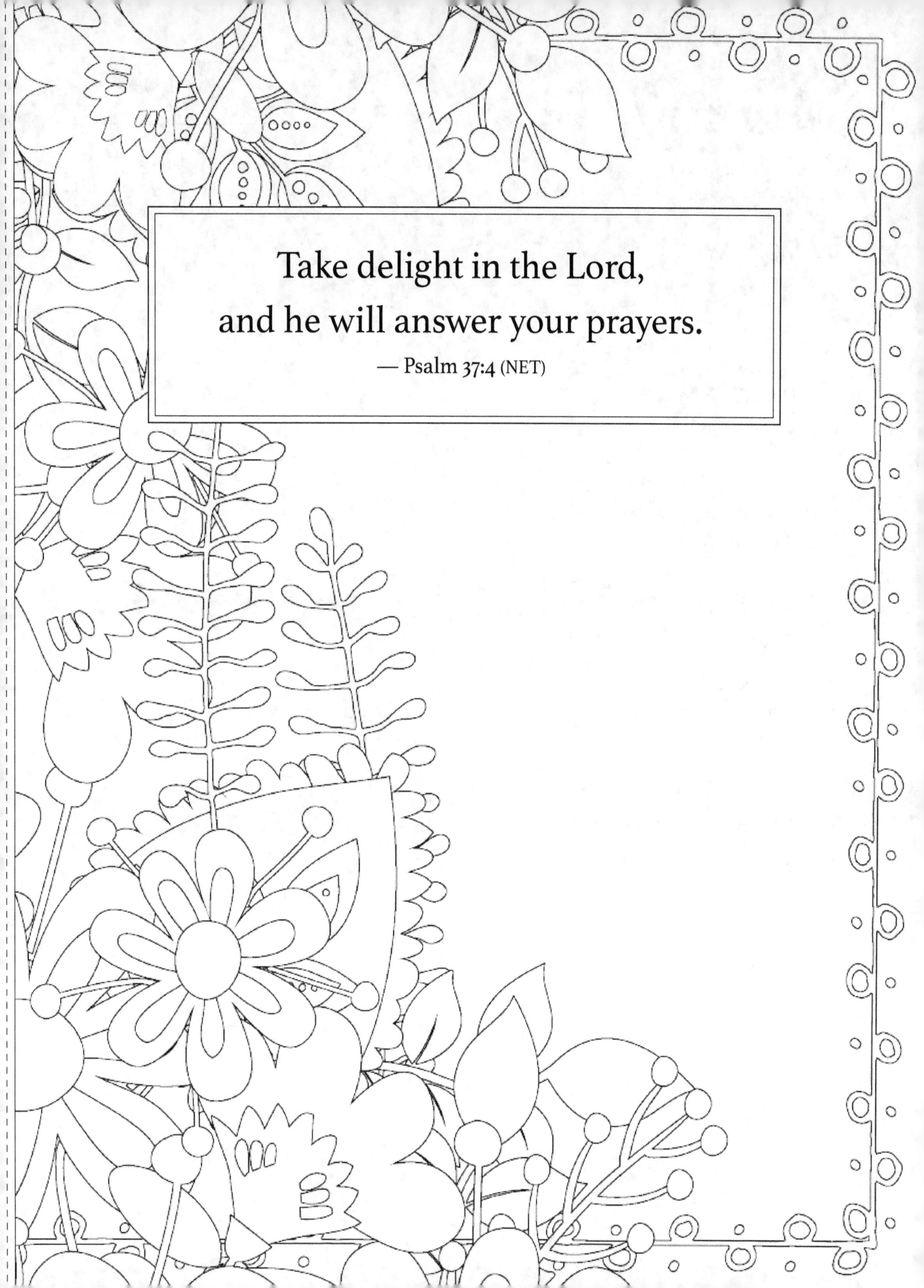

Take delight in the Lord,
and he will answer your prayers.
— Psalm 37:4 (NET)

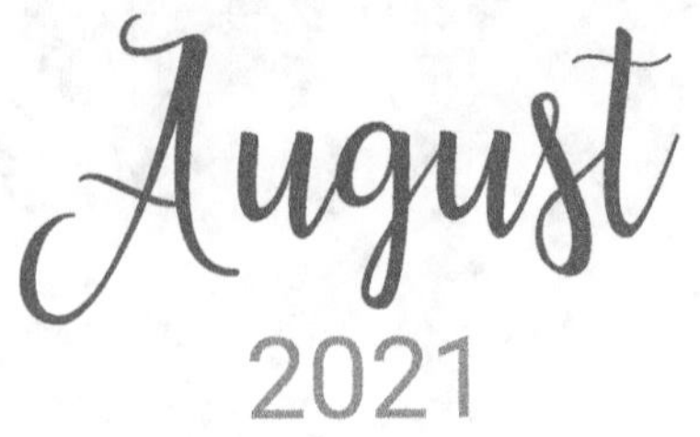

August
2021

<table>
<tr><td colspan="8" align="center">August</td></tr>
<tr><td>S</td><td>M</td><td>T</td><td>W</td><td>T</td><td>F</td><td>S</td></tr>
<tr><td>1</td><td>2</td><td>3</td><td>4</td><td>5</td><td>6</td><td>7</td></tr>
<tr><td>8</td><td>9</td><td>10</td><td>11</td><td>12</td><td>13</td><td>14</td></tr>
<tr><td>15</td><td>16</td><td>17</td><td>18</td><td>19</td><td>20</td><td>21</td></tr>
<tr><td>22</td><td>23</td><td>24</td><td>25</td><td>26</td><td>27</td><td>28</td></tr>
<tr><td>29</td><td>30</td><td>31</td><td></td><td></td><td></td><td></td></tr>
</table>

09 MONDAY

10 TUESDAY

11 WEDNESDAY

12 THURSDAY

13 FRIDAY

14 SATURDAY

15 SUNDAY

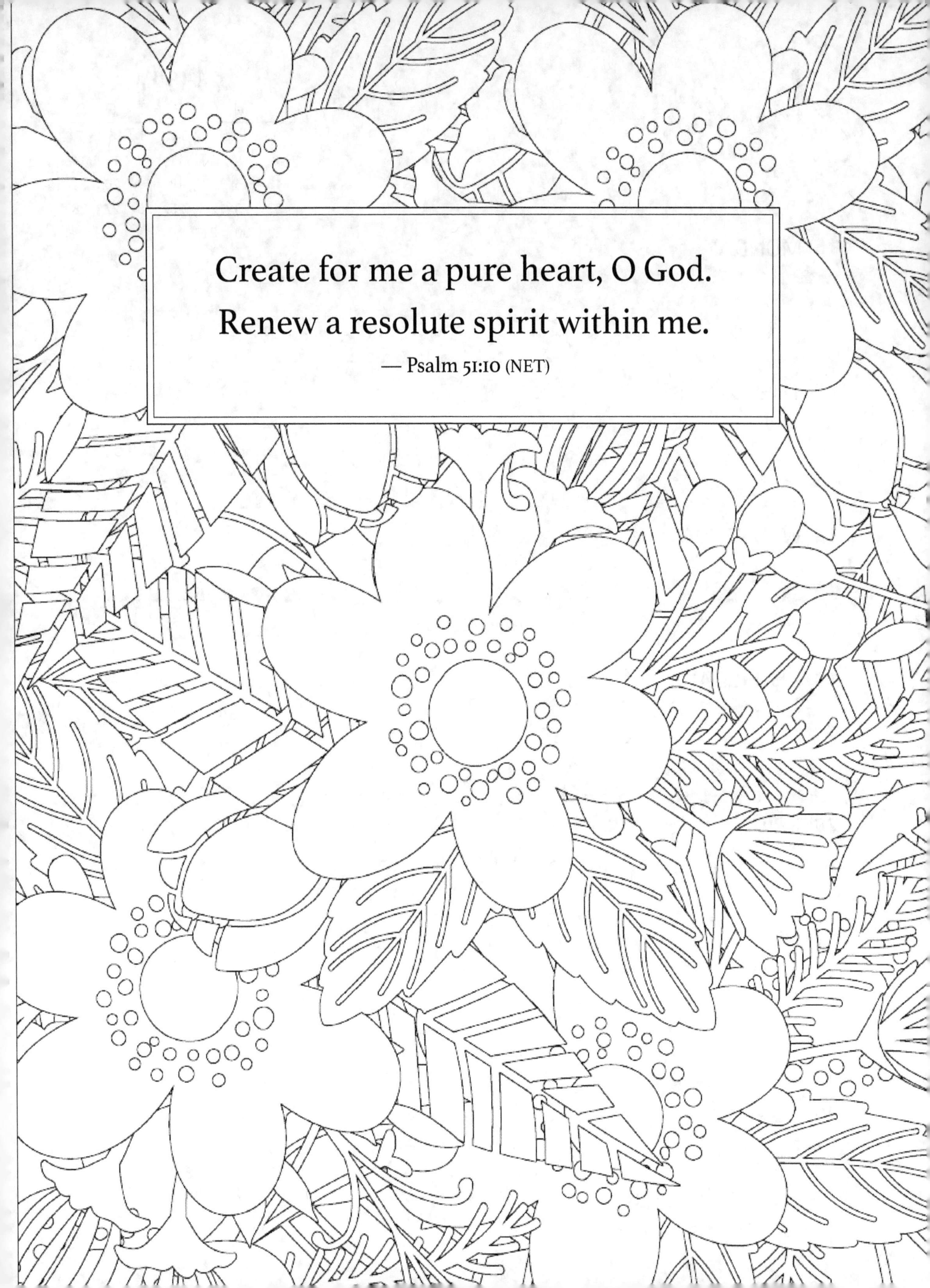

Create for me a pure heart, O God.

Renew a resolute spirit within me.

— Psalm 51:10 (NET)

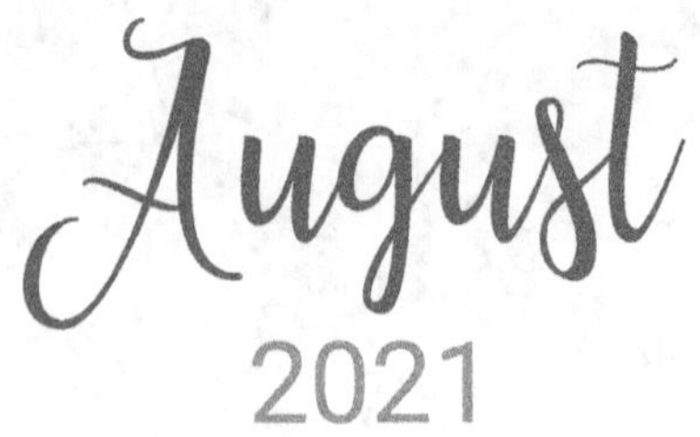

August
2021

16 MONDAY

17 TUESDAY

18 WEDNESDAY

19 THURSDAY

20 FRIDAY

21 SATURDAY

22 SUNDAY

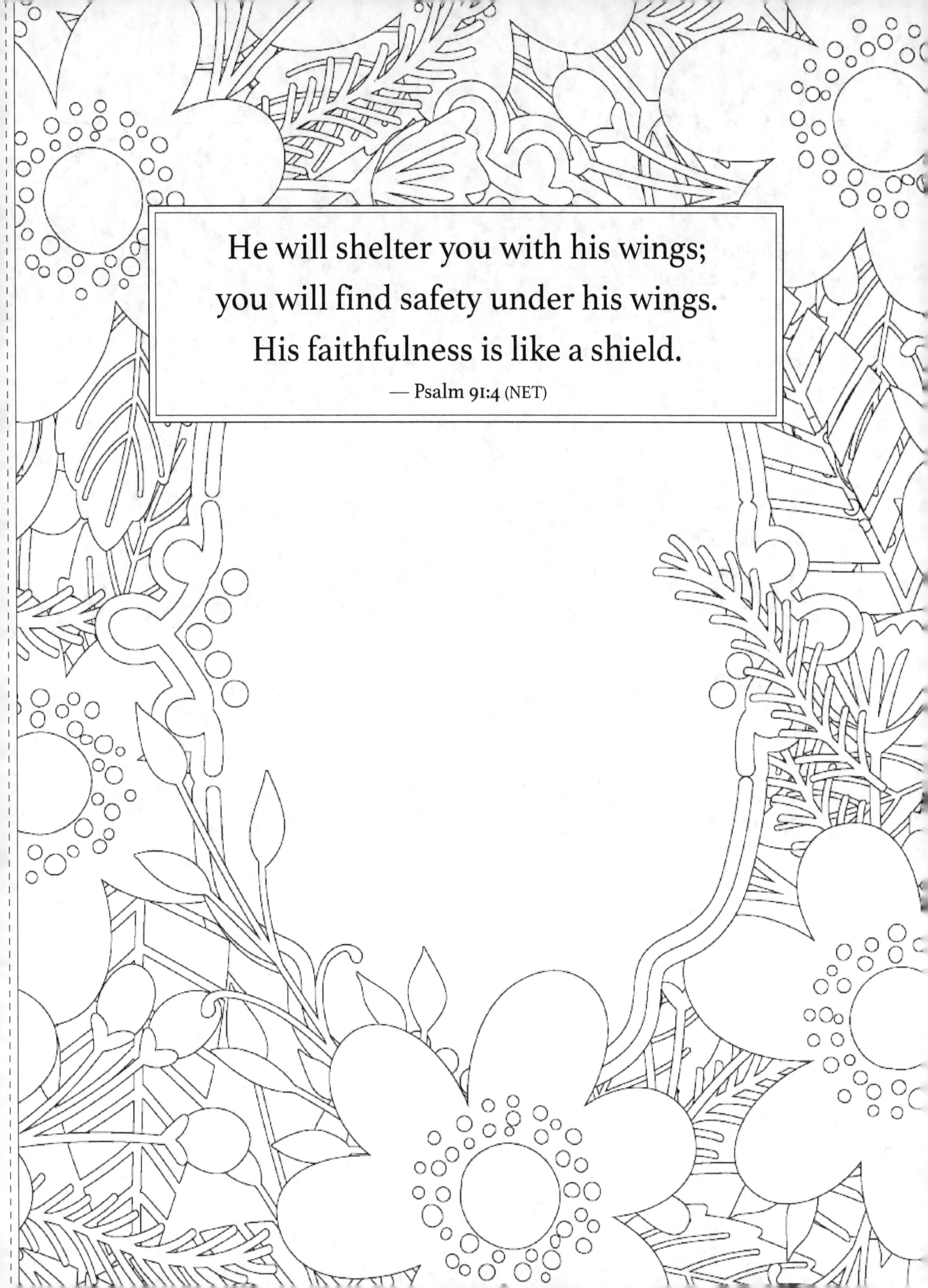
He will shelter you with his wings;
you will find safety under his wings.
His faithfulness is like a shield.
— Psalm 91:4 (NET)

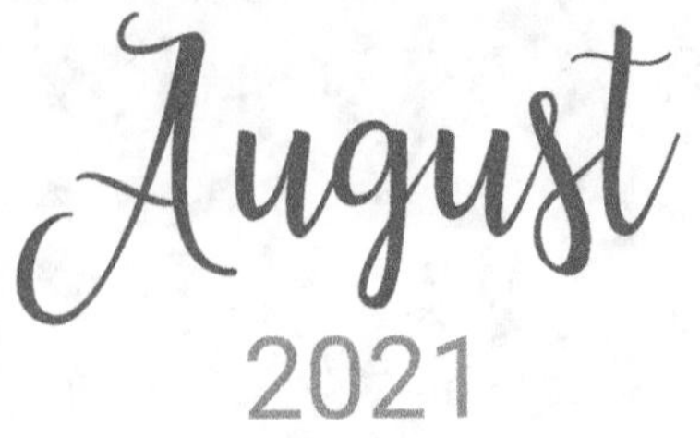

August
2021

23 MONDAY

24 TUESDAY

25 WEDNESDAY

26 THURSDAY

27 FRIDAY

28 SATURDAY

29 SUNDAY

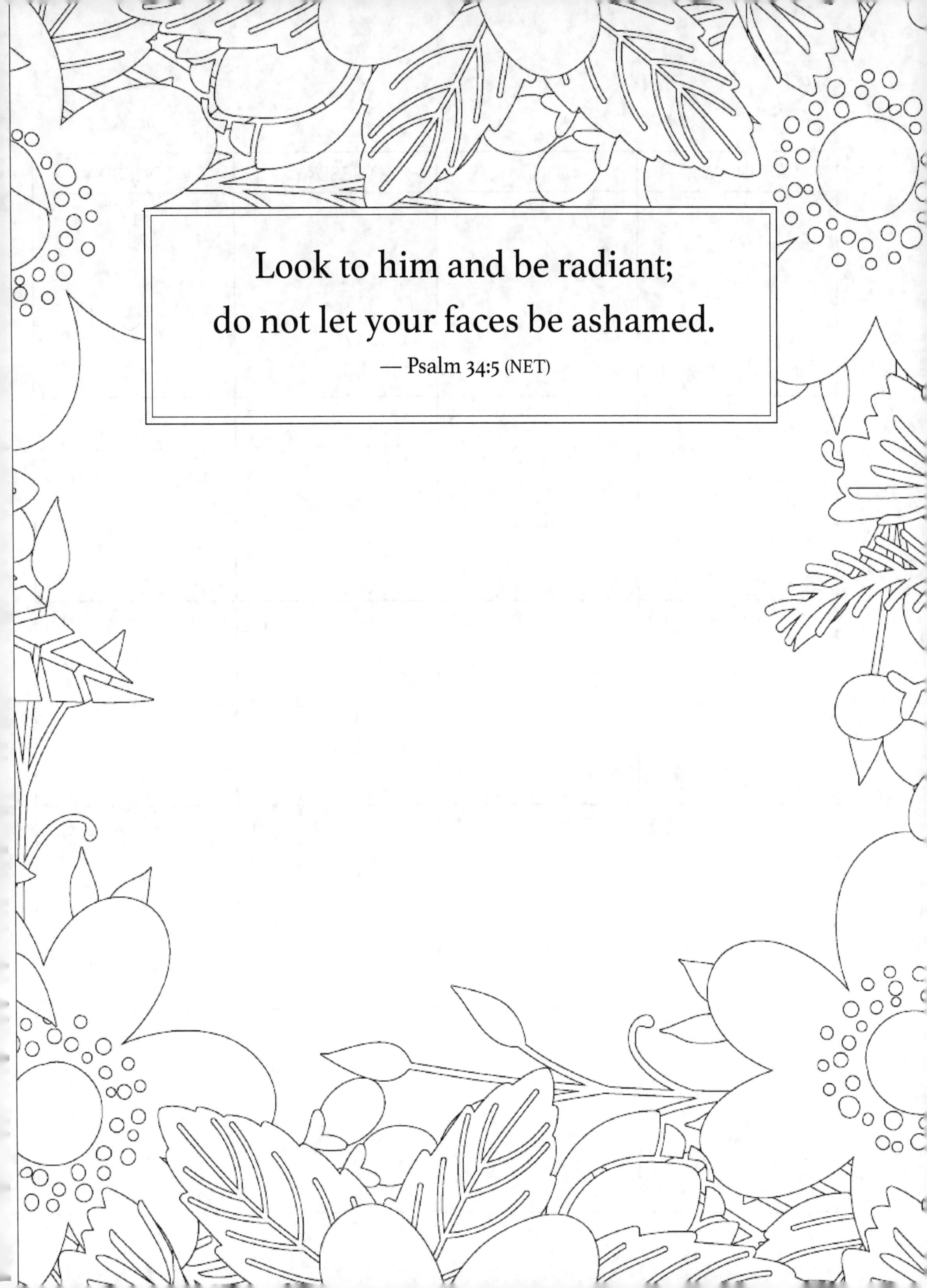

Look to him and be radiant;
do not let your faces be ashamed.
— Psalm 34:5 (NET)

September 2021

SUNDAY	MONDAY	TUESDAY	WEDNESDAY
			1
5	6 Labor Day Rosh Hashanah Begins	7 Rosh Hashanah Ends	8
12	13	14	15 Yom Kippur Begins
19	20	21	22 First Day of Autumn
26	27	28	29

September 2021

THURSDAY	FRIDAY	SATURDAY	NOTES
2	3	4	○
			○
			○
			○
			○
9	10	11	○
			○
			○
			○
			○
16 Yom Kippur Ends	17	18	○
			○
			○
			○
23	24	25	○
			○
			○
			○
			○
30			NOTES

September
2021

30 MONDAY

31 TUESDAY

01 WEDNESDAY

02 THURSDAY

03 FRIDAY

04 SATURDAY

05 SUNDAY

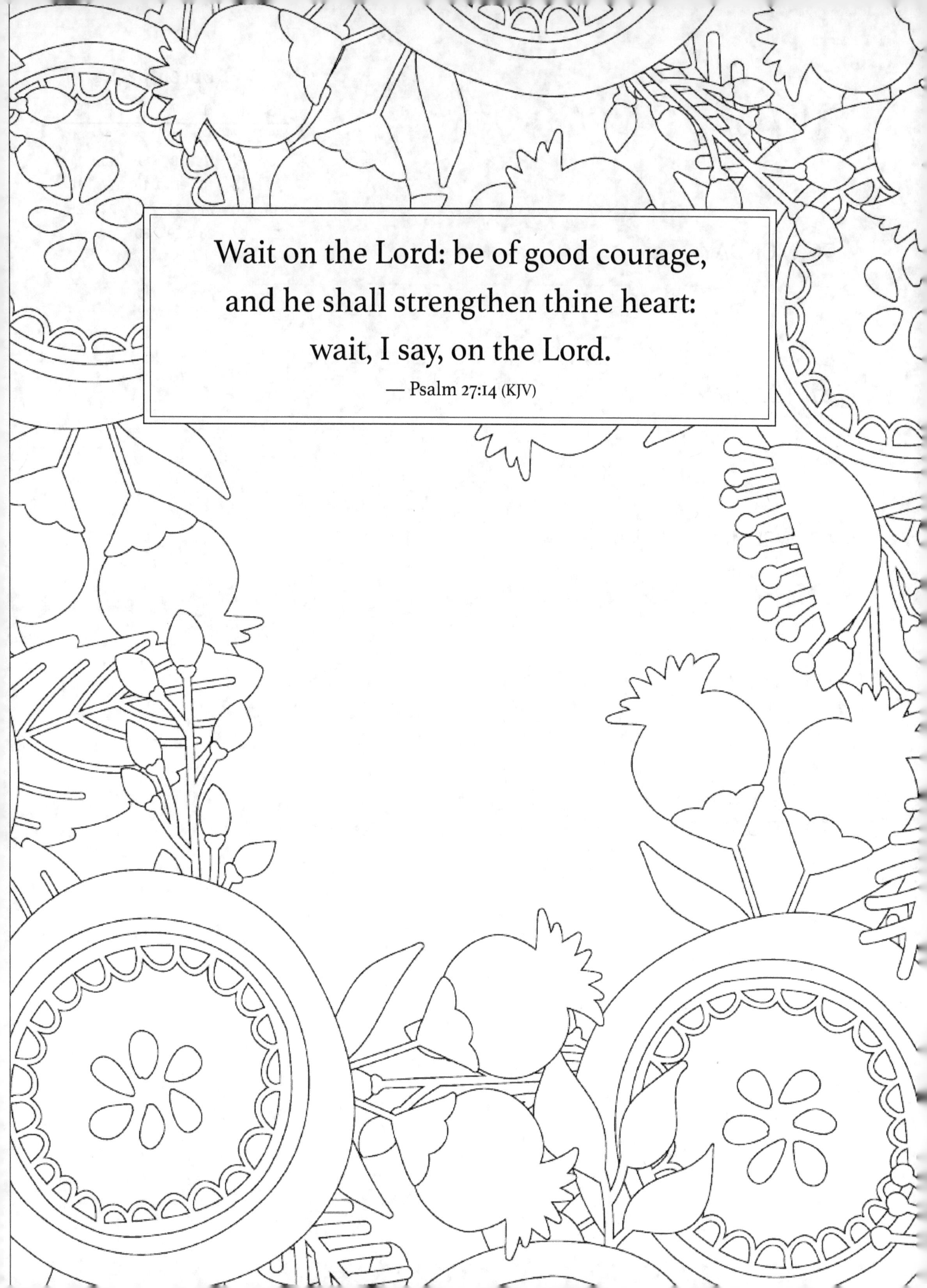

Wait on the Lord: be of good courage,
and he shall strengthen thine heart:
wait, I say, on the Lord.
— Psalm 27:14 (KJV)

September

2021

06 MONDAY   Labor Day / Rosh Hashanah Begins

07 TUESDAY

08 WEDNESDAY   Rosh Hashanah Ends

09 THURSDAY

10 FRIDAY

11 SATURDAY

12 SUNDAY

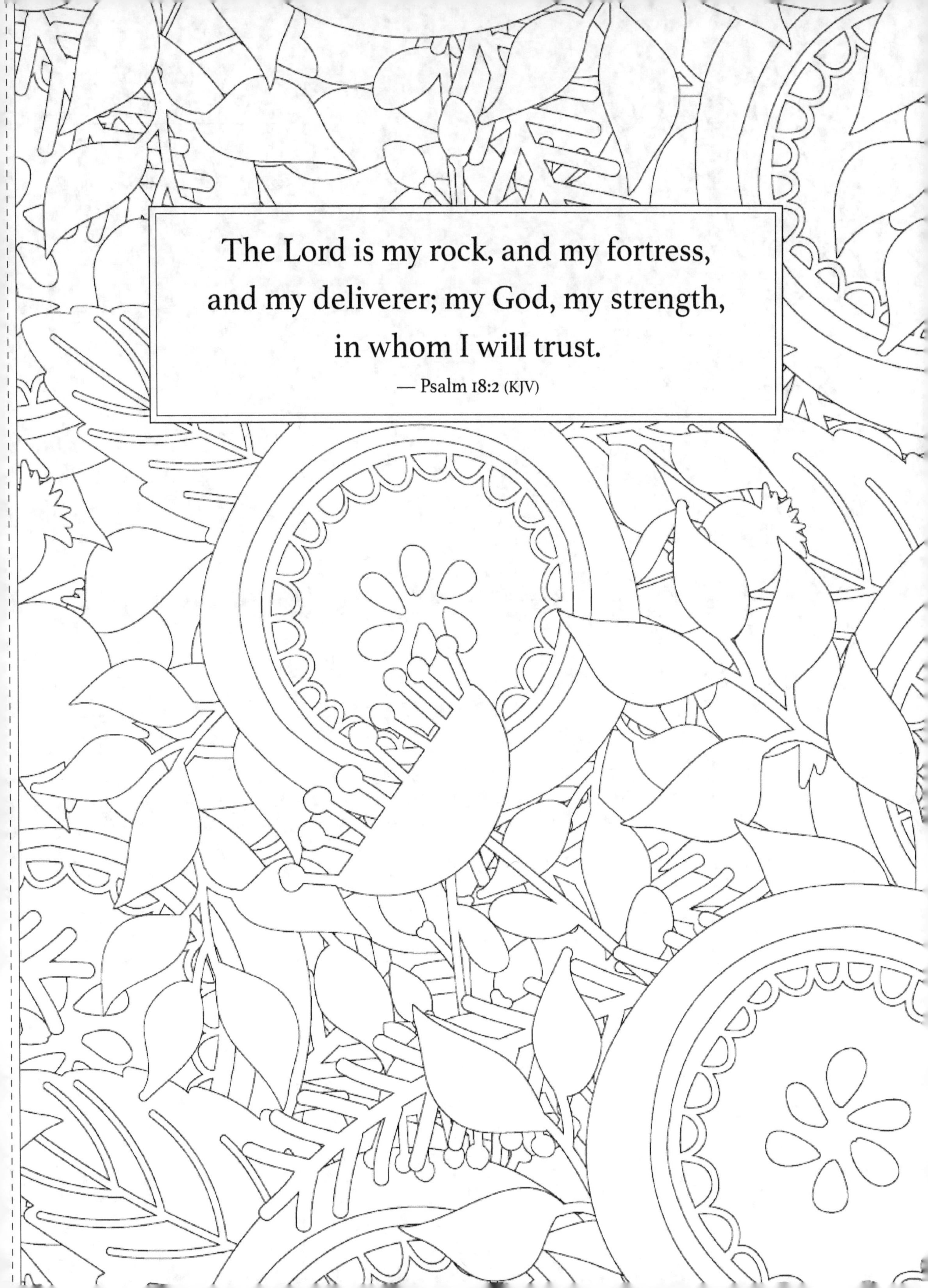

The Lord is my rock, and my fortress,
and my deliverer; my God, my strength,
in whom I will trust.
— Psalm 18:2 (KJV)

September

2021

13 MONDAY

14 TUESDAY

15 WEDNESDAY   Yom Kippur Begins

16 THURSDAY   Yom Kippur Ends

17 FRIDAY

18 SATURDAY

19 SUNDAY

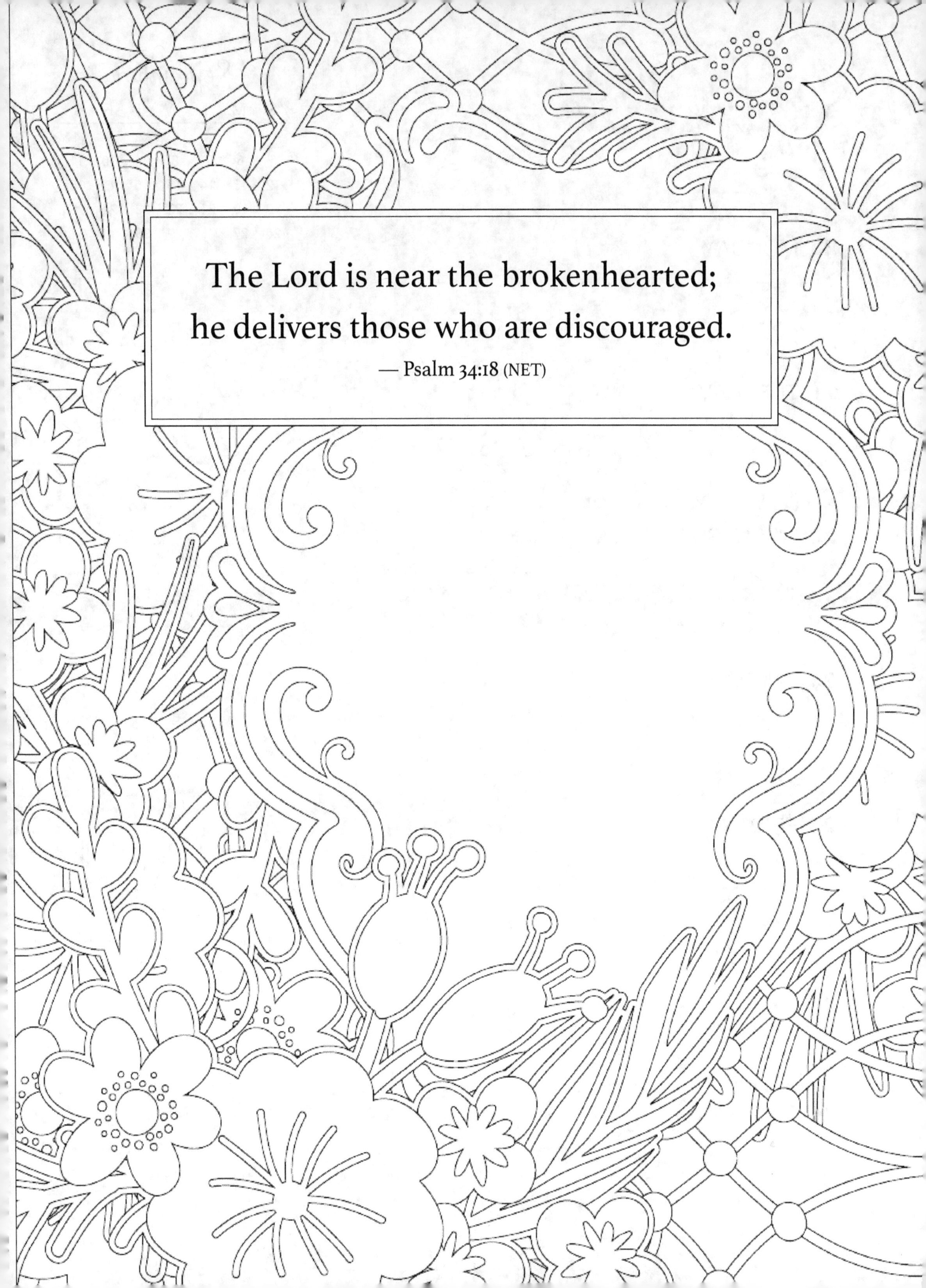

The Lord is near the brokenhearted;
he delivers those who are discouraged.
— Psalm 34:18 (NET)

September

2021

20 MONDAY

21 TUESDAY

22 WEDNESDAY   First Day of Autumn

23 THURSDAY

24 FRIDAY

25 SATURDAY

26 SUNDAY

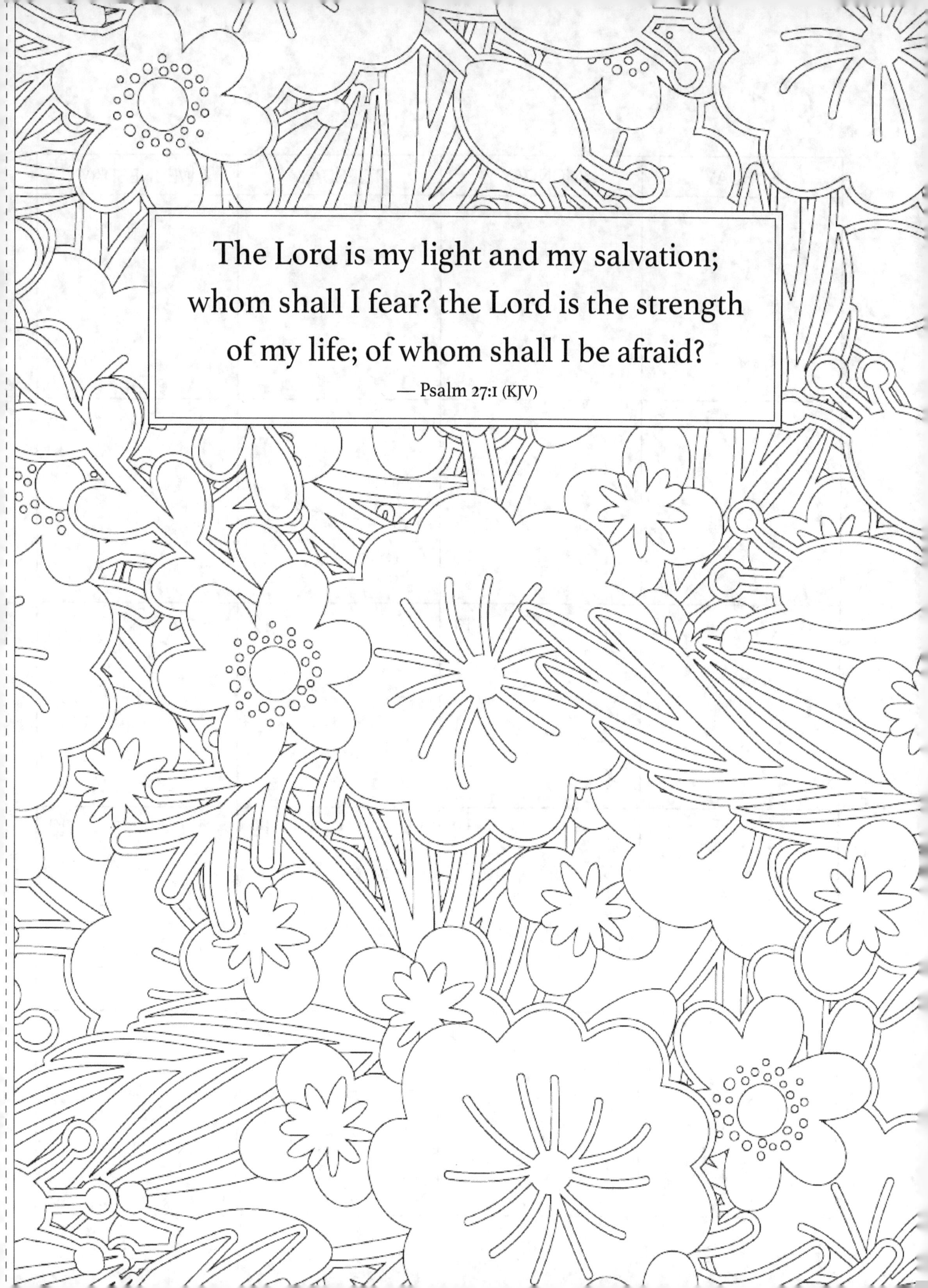

The Lord is my light and my salvation;
whom shall I fear? the Lord is the strength
of my life; of whom shall I be afraid?
— Psalm 27:1 (KJV)

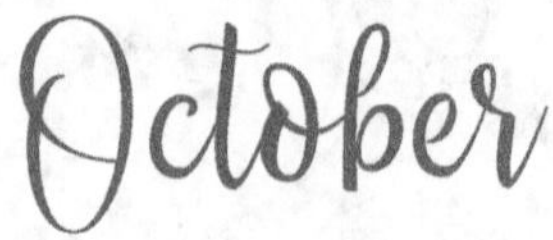

SUNDAY	MONDAY	TUESDAY	WEDNESDAY
3	4	5	6
10	11 Indigenous Peoples' Day	12	13
17	18	19	20
24	25	26	27
31 Halloween			

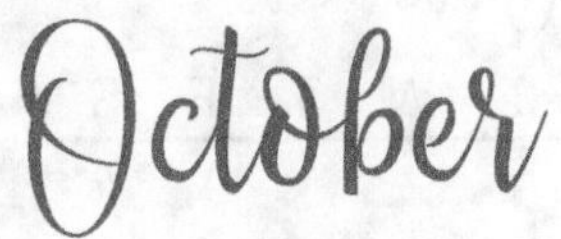

October   2021

THURSDAY	FRIDAY	SATURDAY	NOTES
	1	2	○
			○
			○
			○
			○
7	8	9	○
			○
			○
			○
14	15	16	○
			○
			○
			○
			○
21	22	23	○
			○
			○
			○
			○
28	29	30	NOTES

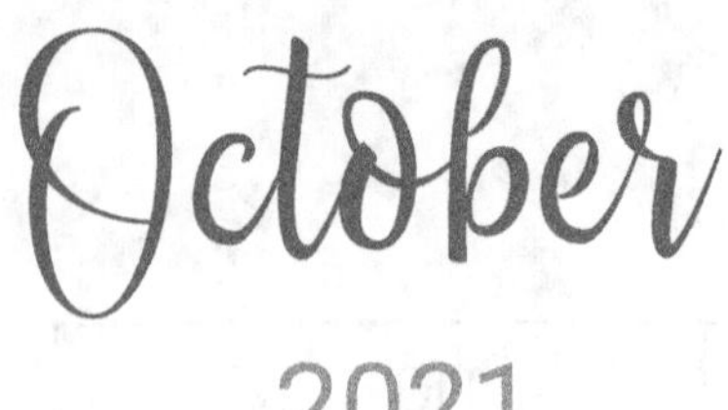

October

2021

27 MONDAY

28 TUESDAY

29 WEDNESDAY

30 THURSDAY

01 FRIDAY

02 SATURDAY

03 SUNDAY

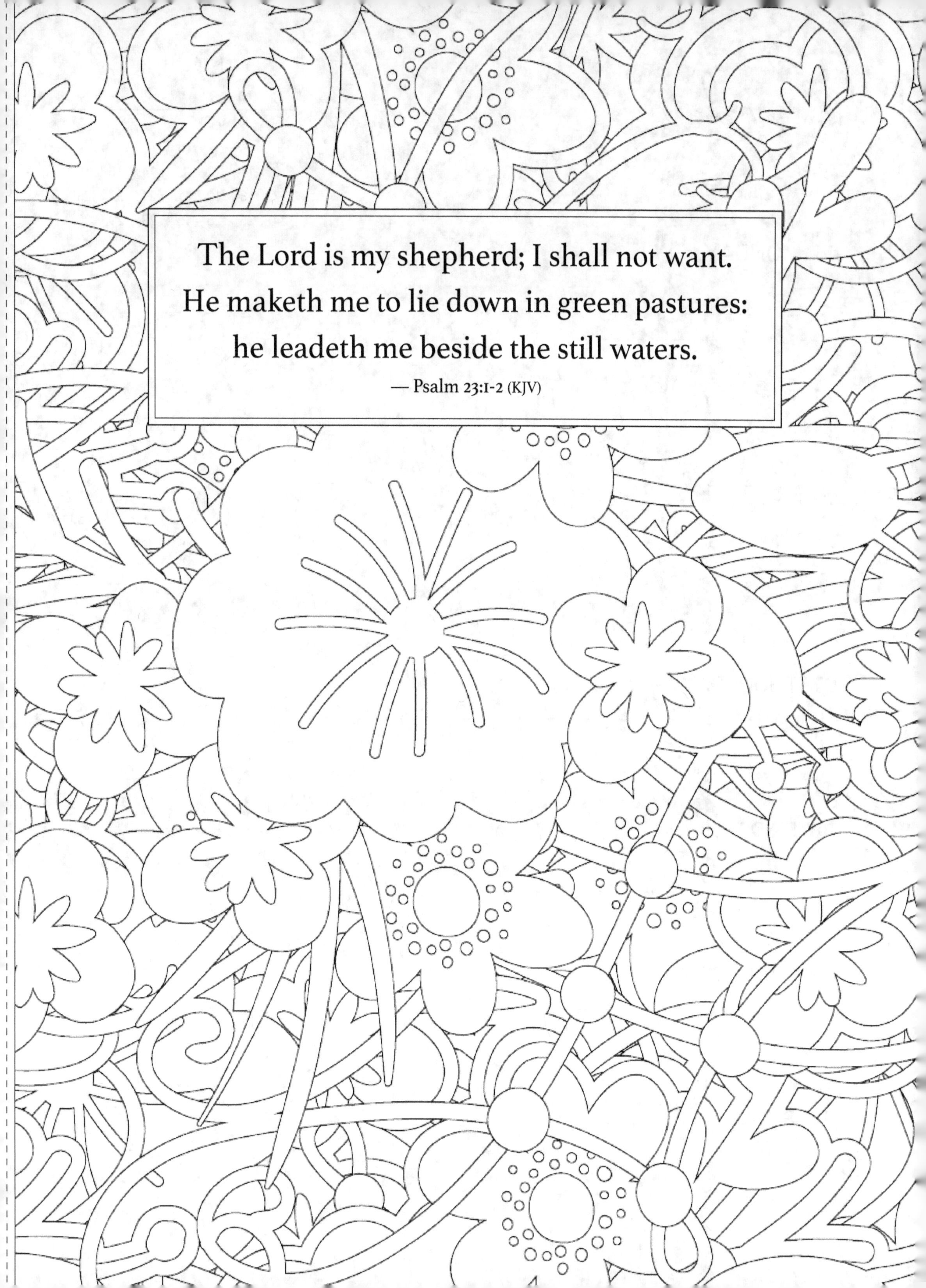

The Lord is my shepherd; I shall not want.
He maketh me to lie down in green pastures:
he leadeth me beside the still waters.
— Psalm 23:1-2 (KJV)

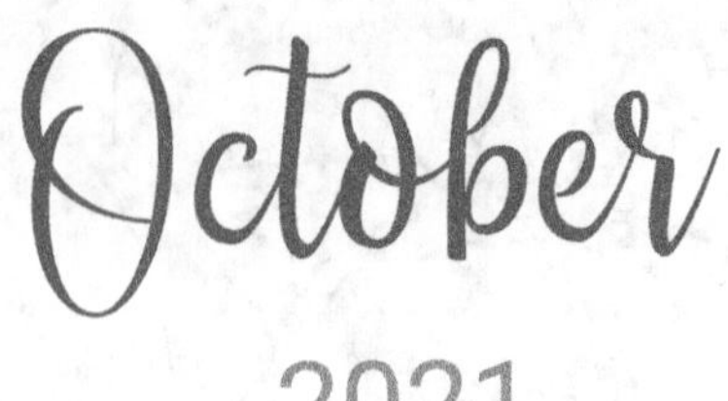

October

2021

04 MONDAY

05 TUESDAY

06 WEDNESDAY

07 THURSDAY

08 FRIDAY

09 SATURDAY

10 SUNDAY

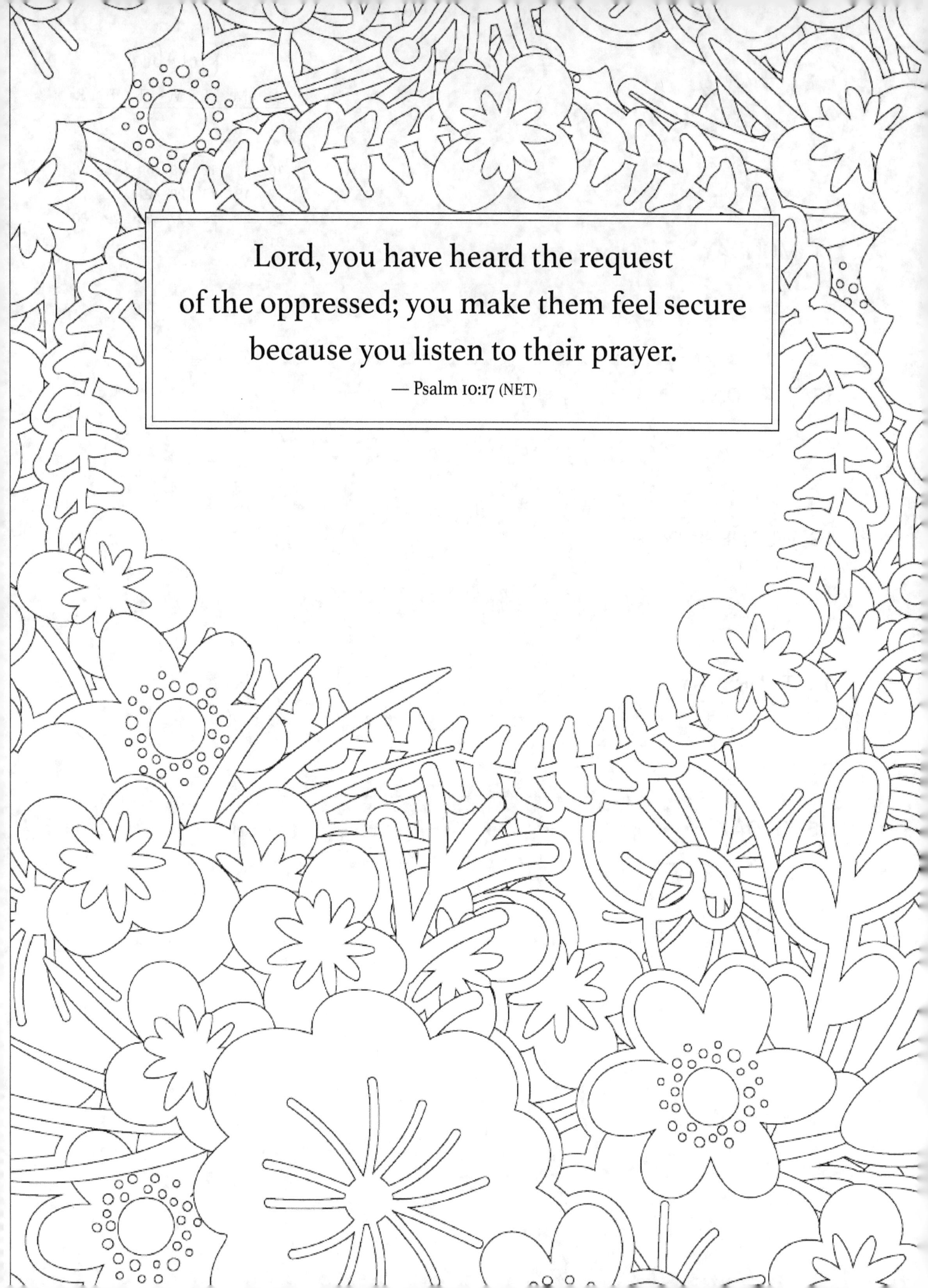

Lord, you have heard the request
of the oppressed; you make them feel secure
because you listen to their prayer.
— Psalm 10:17 (NET)

October

2021

11 MONDAY   Indigenous Peoples' Day

12 TUESDAY

13 WEDNESDAY

14 THURSDAY

15 FRIDAY

16 SATURDAY

17 SUNDAY

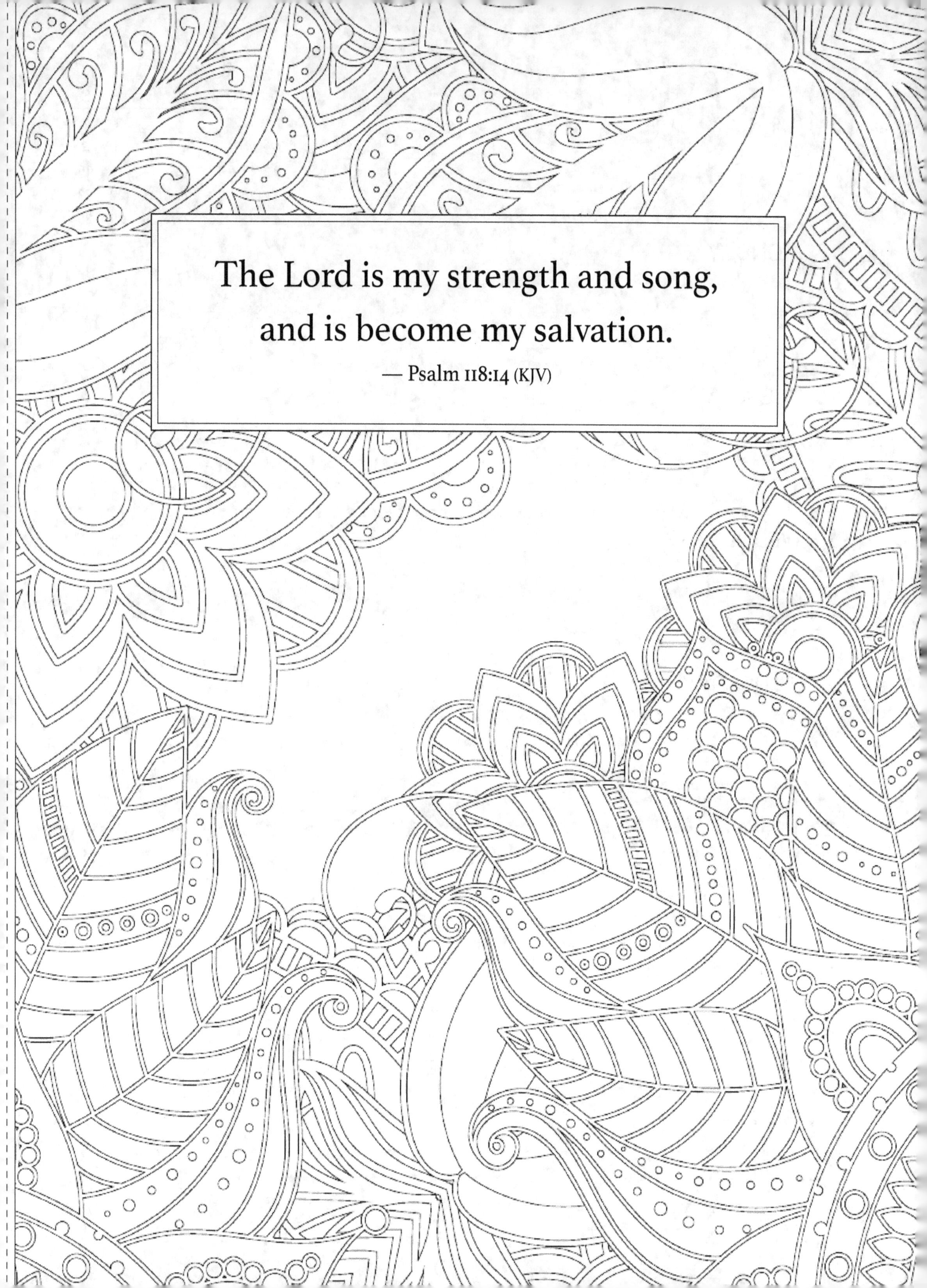

The Lord is my strength and song,
and is become my salvation.
— Psalm 118:14 (KJV)

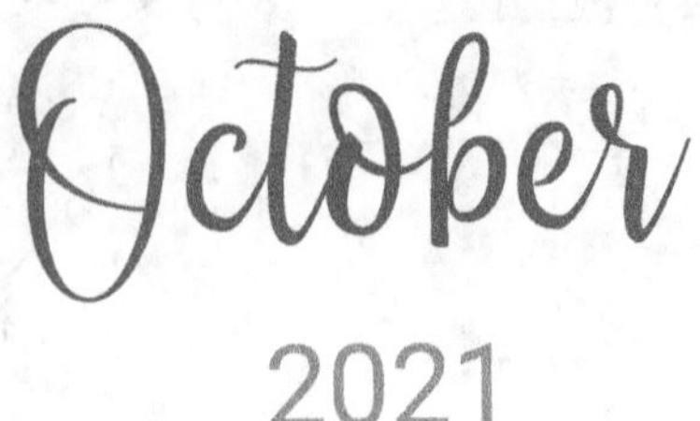

October

2021

18 MONDAY

19 TUESDAY

20 WEDNESDAY

21 THURSDAY

22 FRIDAY

23 SATURDAY

24 SUNDAY

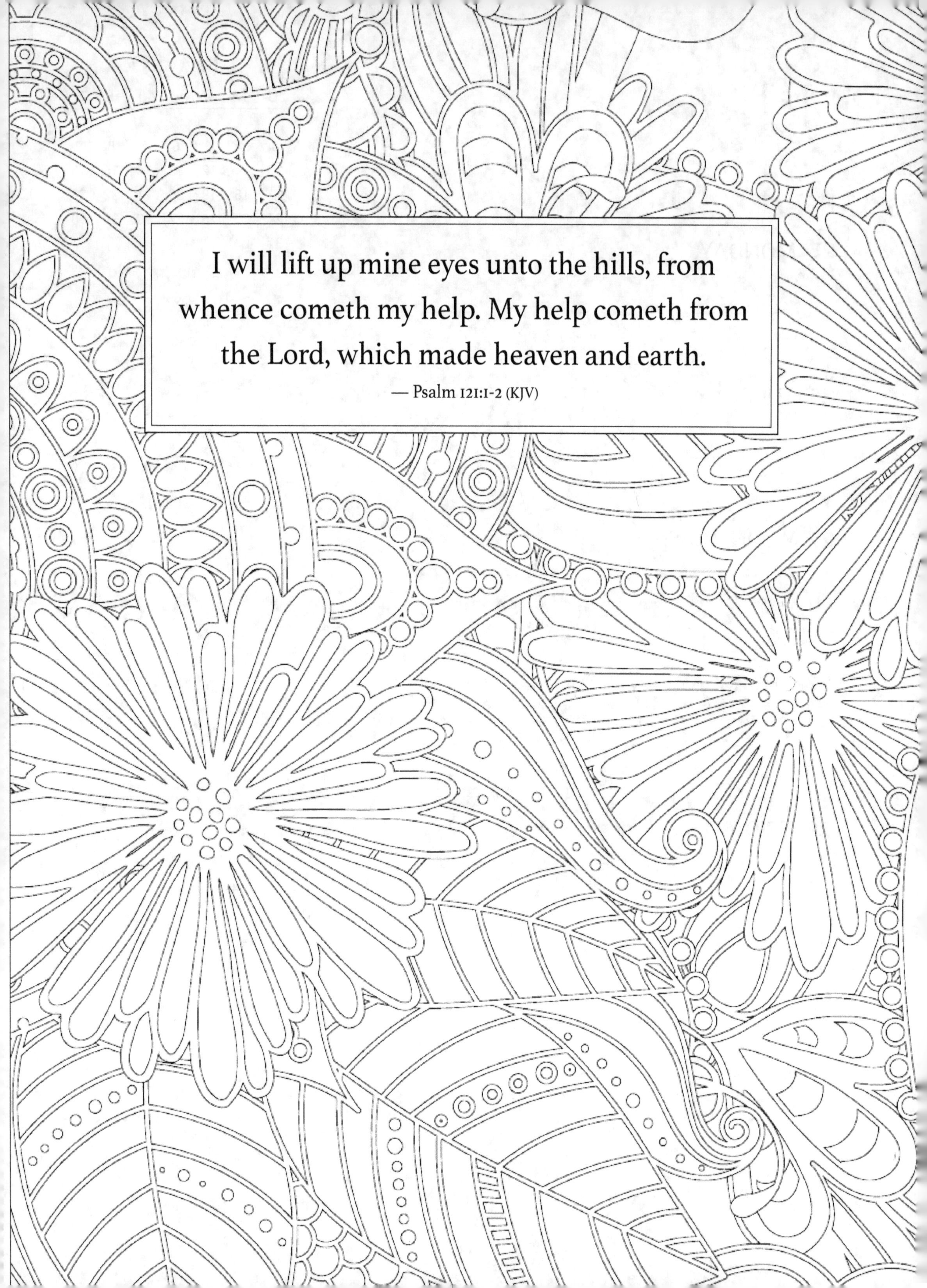

I will lift up mine eyes unto the hills, from whence cometh my help. My help cometh from the Lord, which made heaven and earth.
— Psalm 121:1-2 (KJV)

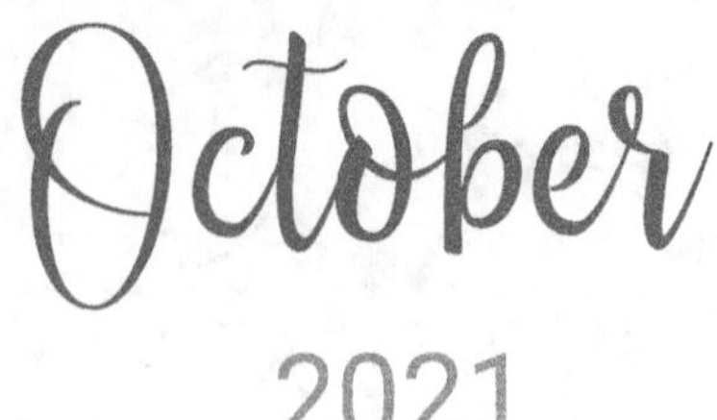

October

2021

25 MONDAY

26 TUESDAY

27 WEDNESDAY

28 THURSDAY

29 FRIDAY

30 SATURDAY

31 SUNDAY   Halloween

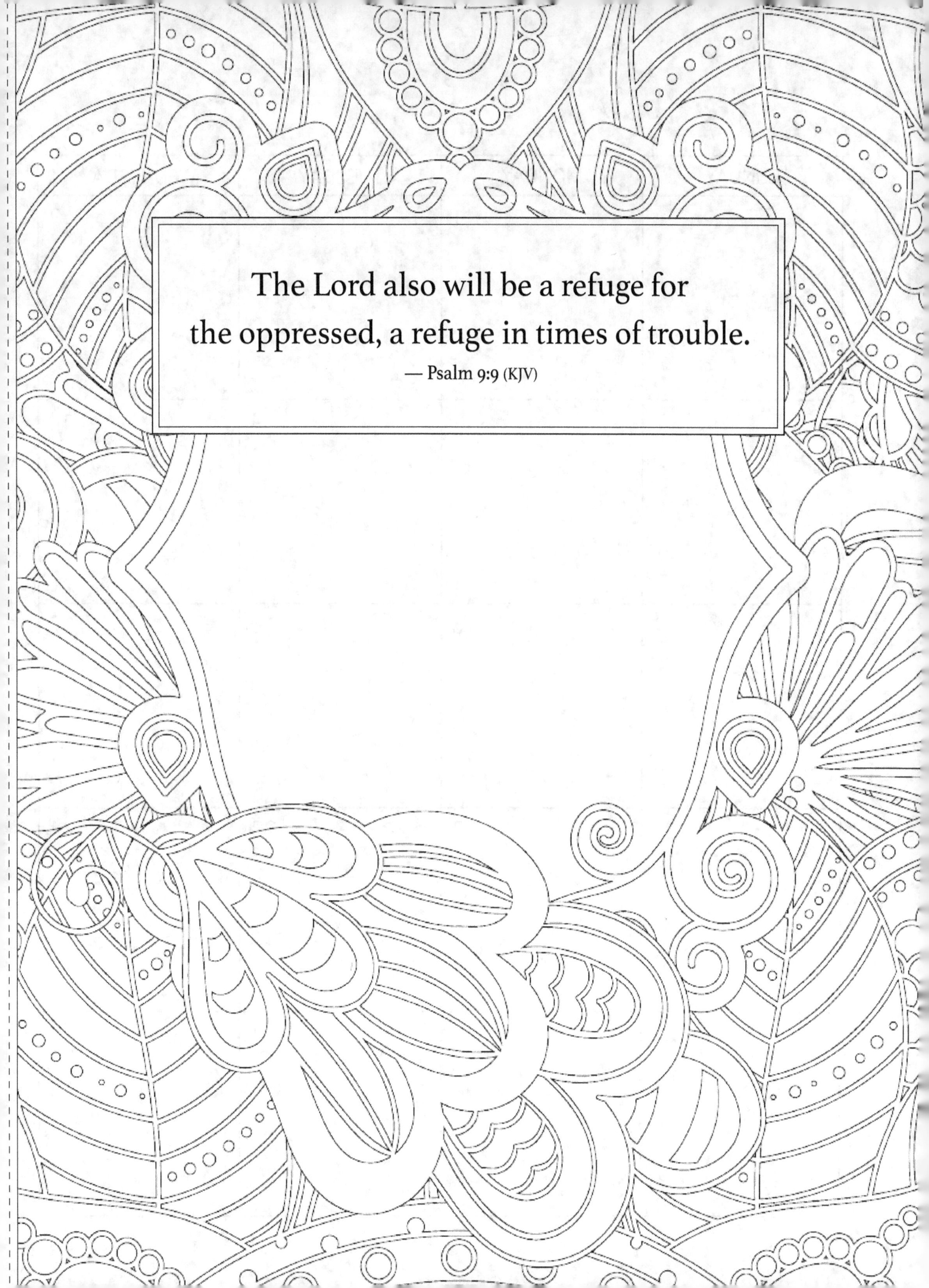

The Lord also will be a refuge for
the oppressed, a refuge in times of trouble.
— Psalm 9:9 (KJV)

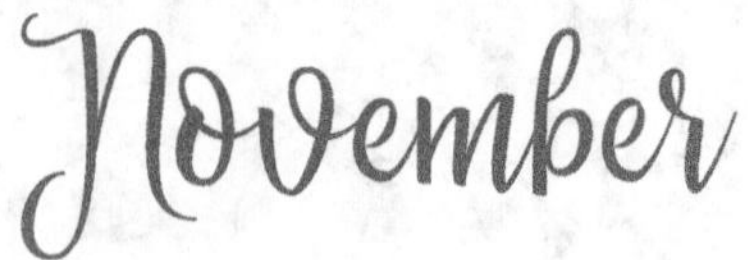

November 2021

SUNDAY	MONDAY	TUESDAY	WEDNESDAY
	1	2	3
7 Daylight Saving Time Ends	8	9	10
14	15	16	17
21	22	23	24
28 Hanukkah Begins	29	30	

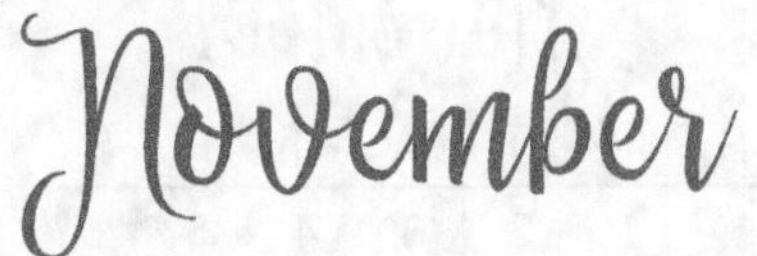

November 2021

THURSDAY	FRIDAY	SATURDAY	NOTES
4	5	6	○
			○
			○
			○
			○
11 Veterans Day	12	13	○
			○
			○
			○
18	19	20	○
			○
			○
			○
25 Thanksgiving	26	27	○
			○
			○
			○
			○
			NOTES

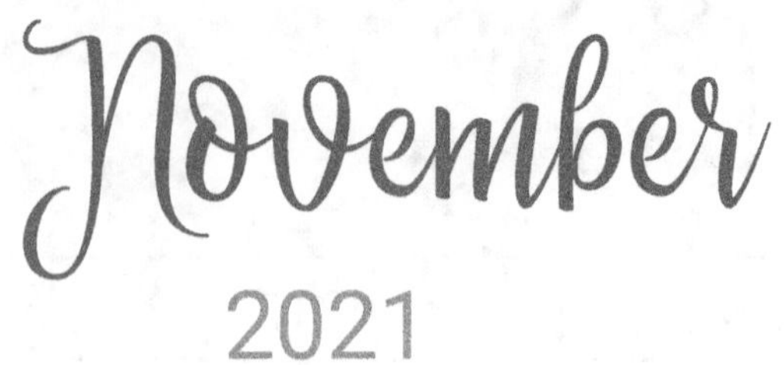

November

2021

01 MONDAY

02 TUESDAY

03 WEDNESDAY

04 THURSDAY

05 FRIDAY

06 SATURDAY

07 SUNDAY   Daylight Saving Time Ends

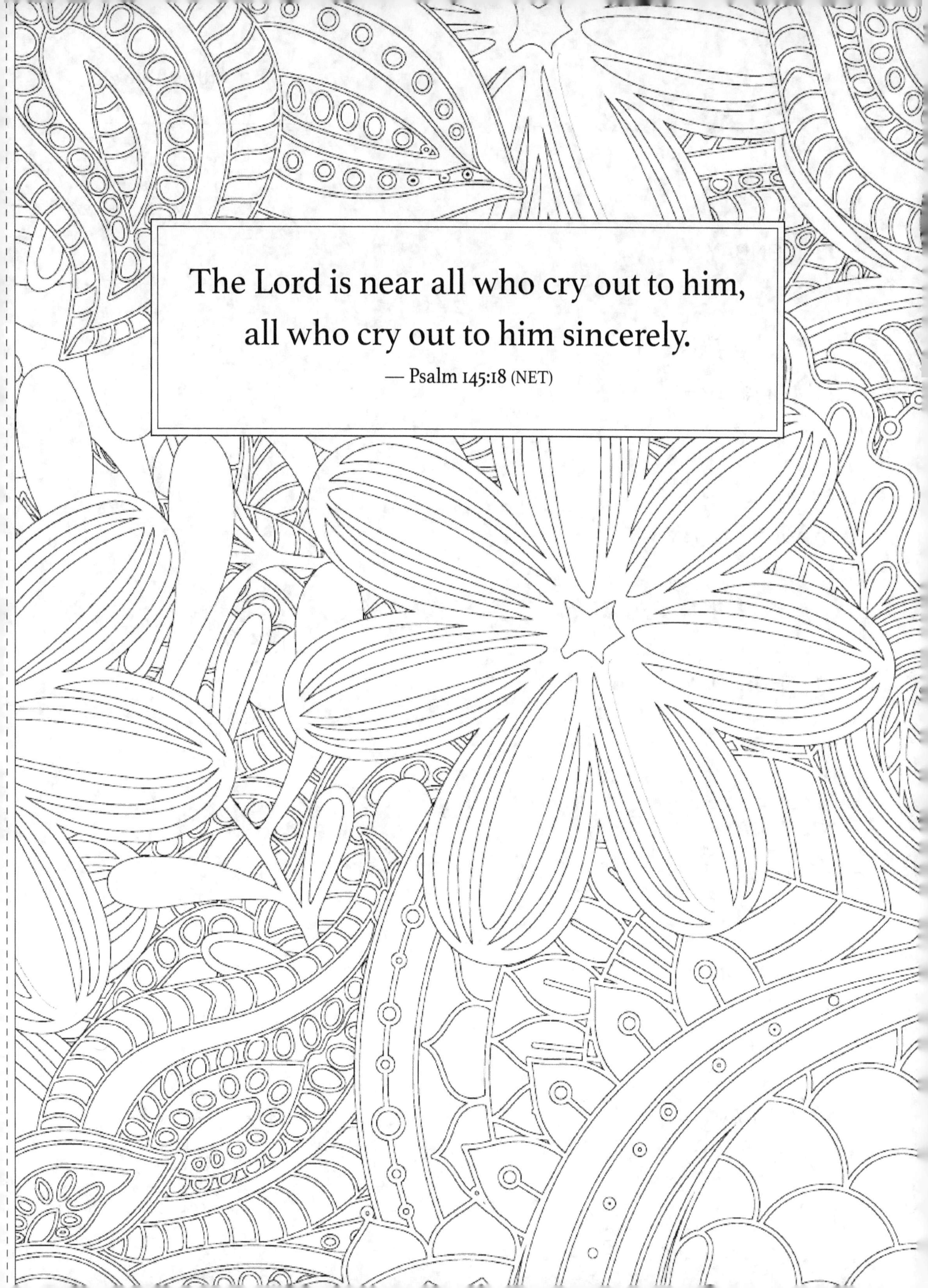
The Lord is near all who cry out to him,
all who cry out to him sincerely.
— Psalm 145:18 (NET)

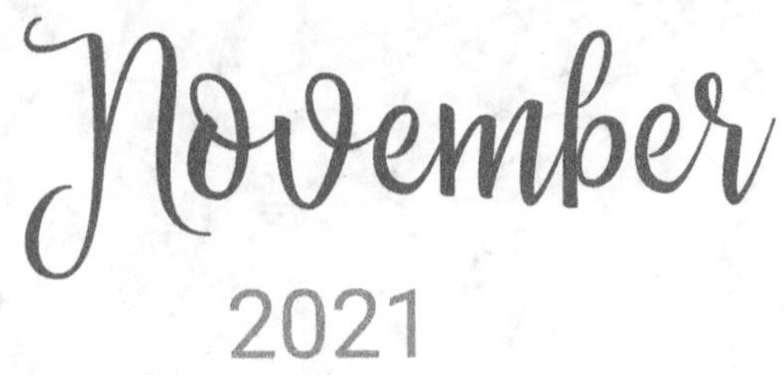

November

2021

08 MONDAY

09 TUESDAY

10 WEDNESDAY

11 THURSDAY Veterans Day

12 FRIDAY

13 SATURDAY

14 SUNDAY

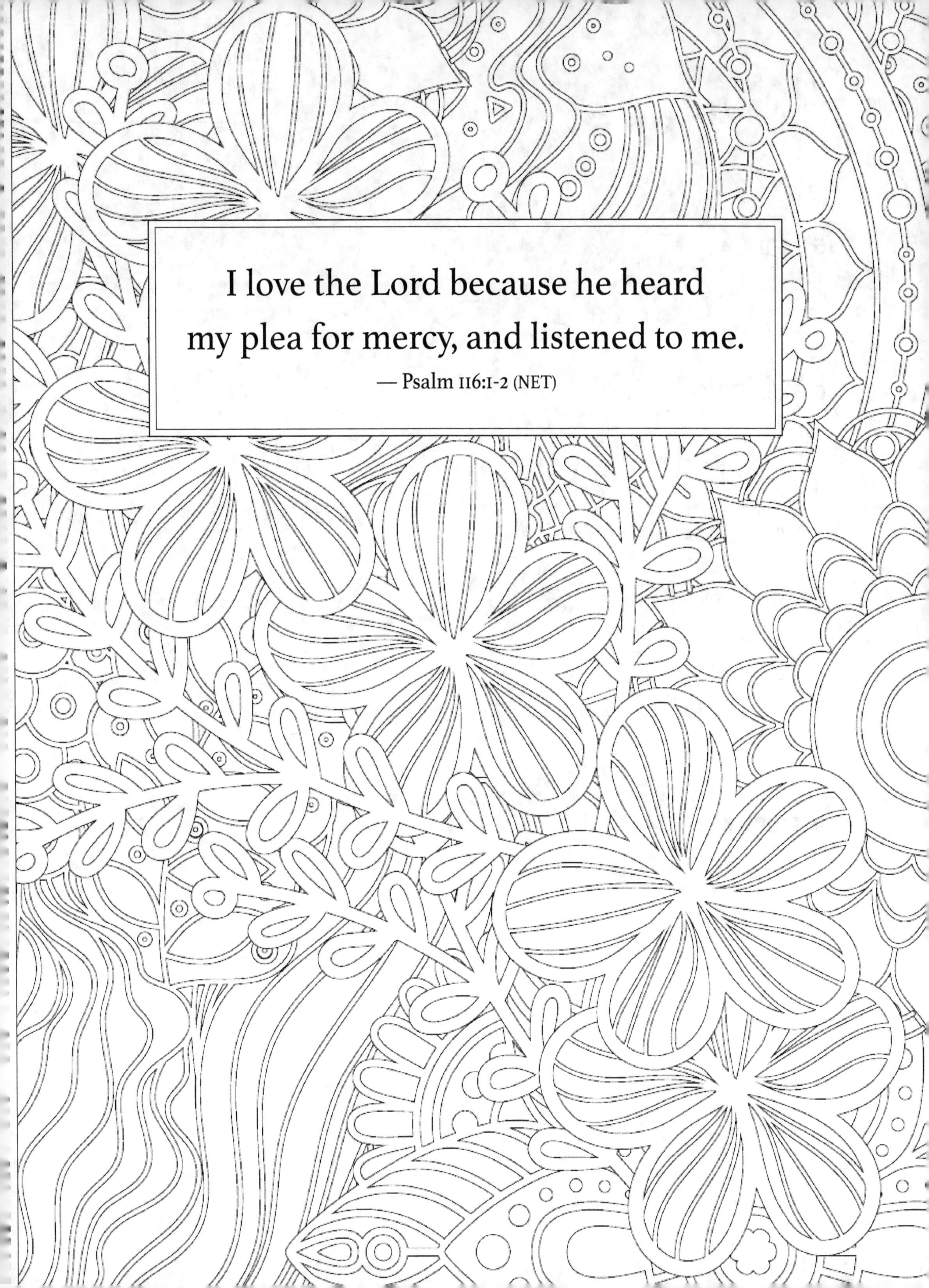

I love the Lord because he heard
my plea for mercy, and listened to me.
— Psalm 116:1-2 (NET)

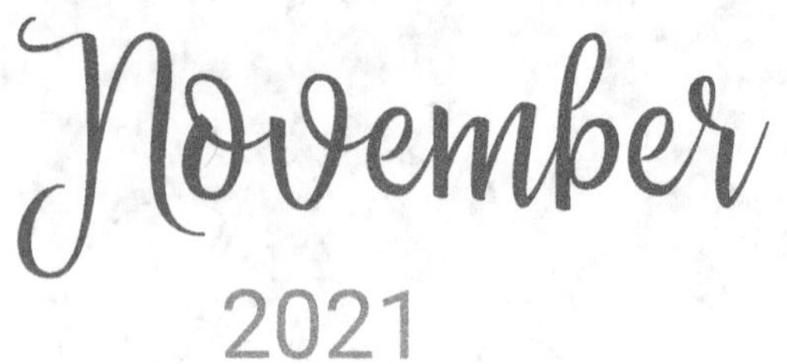

November
2021

15 MONDAY

16 TUESDAY

17 WEDNESDAY

18 THURSDAY

19 FRIDAY

20 SATURDAY

21 SUNDAY

Know ye that the Lord he is God: it is he that
hath made us, and not we ourselves;
we are his people, and the sheep of his pasture.
— Psalm 100:3 (KJV)

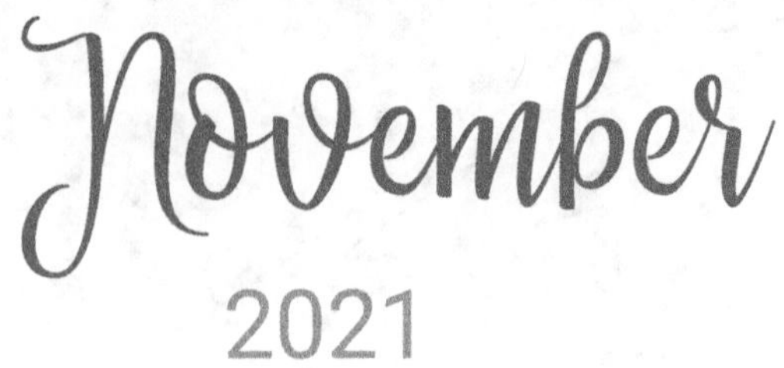

November
2021

22 MONDAY

23 TUESDAY

24 WEDNESDAY

25 THURSDAY   Thanksgiving

26 FRIDAY

27 SATURDAY

28 SUNDAY   Hanukkah Begins

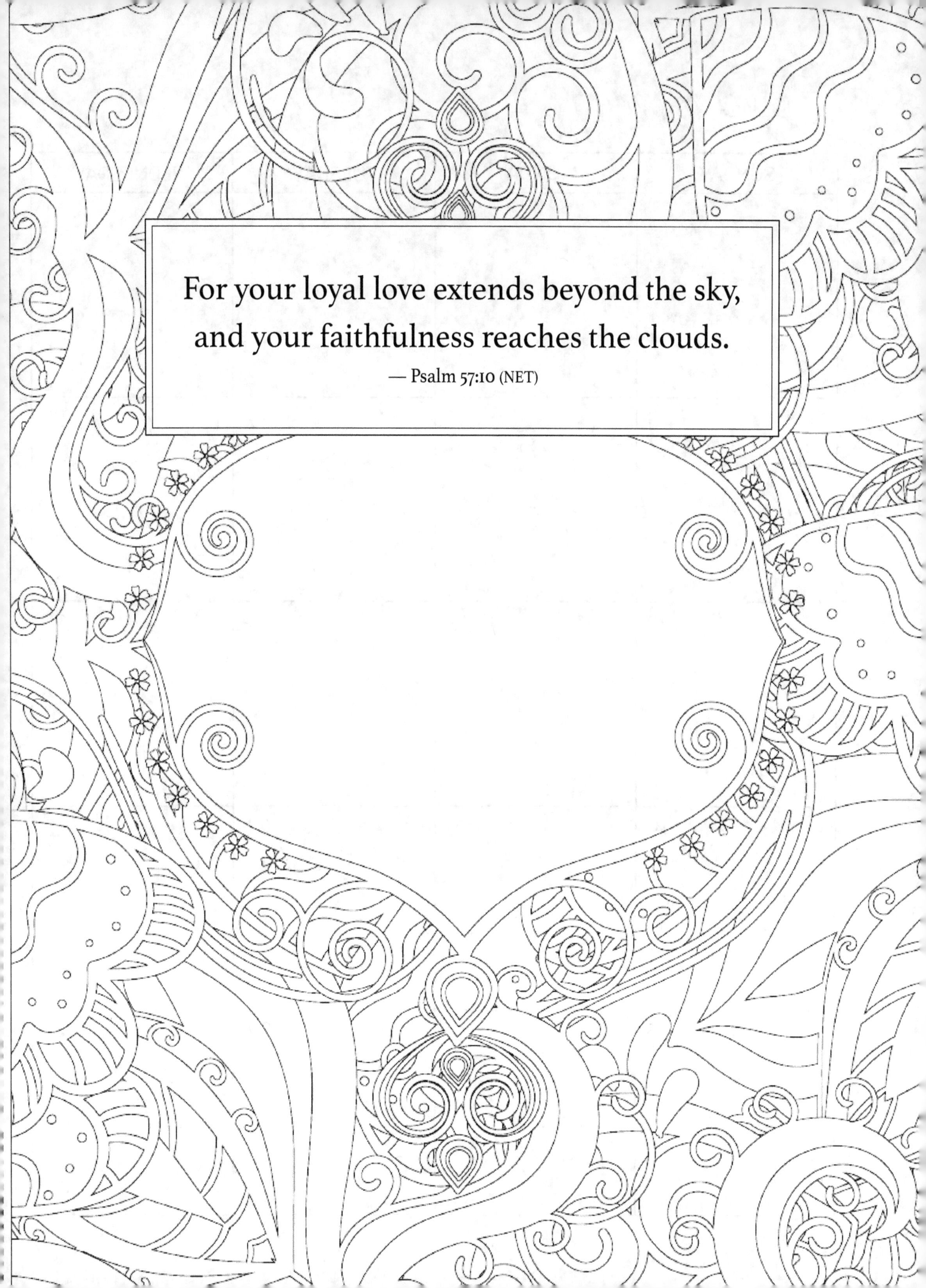

For your loyal love extends beyond the sky,
and your faithfulness reaches the clouds.
— Psalm 57:10 (NET)

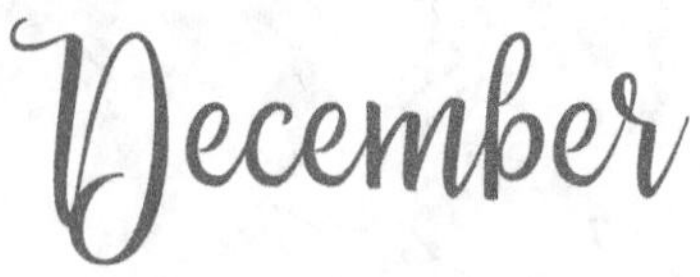

December 2021

SUNDAY	MONDAY	TUESDAY	WEDNESDAY
			1
5	6 Hanukkah Ends	7	8
12	13	14	15
19	20	21 First Day of Winter	22
26	27	28	29

December 2021

THURSDAY	FRIDAY	SATURDAY	NOTES
2	3	4	○
			○
			○
			○
			○
9	10	11	○
			○
			○
			○
16	17	18	○
			○
			○
			○
			○
23	24 Christmas Eve	25 Christmas Day	○
			○
			○
			○
			○
30	31 New Year's Eve		NOTES

December
2021

29 MONDAY

30 TUESDAY

01 WEDNESDAY

02 THURSDAY

03 FRIDAY

04 SATURDAY

05 SUNDAY

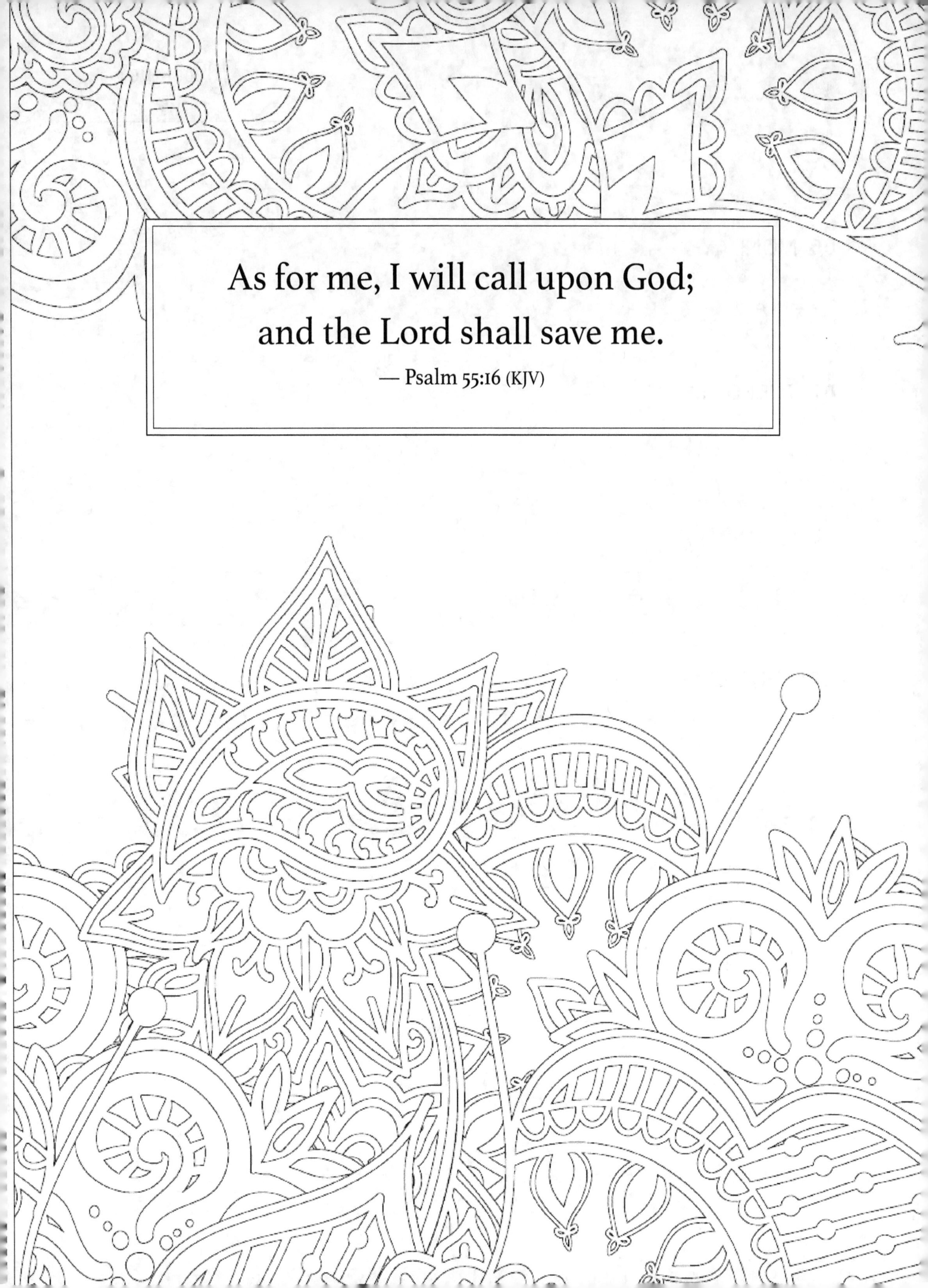
As for me, I will call upon God;
and the Lord shall save me.
— Psalm 55:16 (KJV)

December

2021

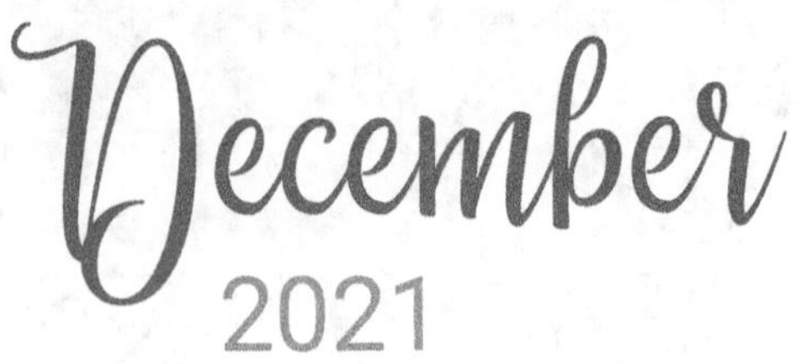

06 MONDAY   Hanukkah Ends

07 TUESDAY

08 WEDNESDAY

09 THURSDAY

10 FRIDAY

11 SATURDAY

12 SUNDAY

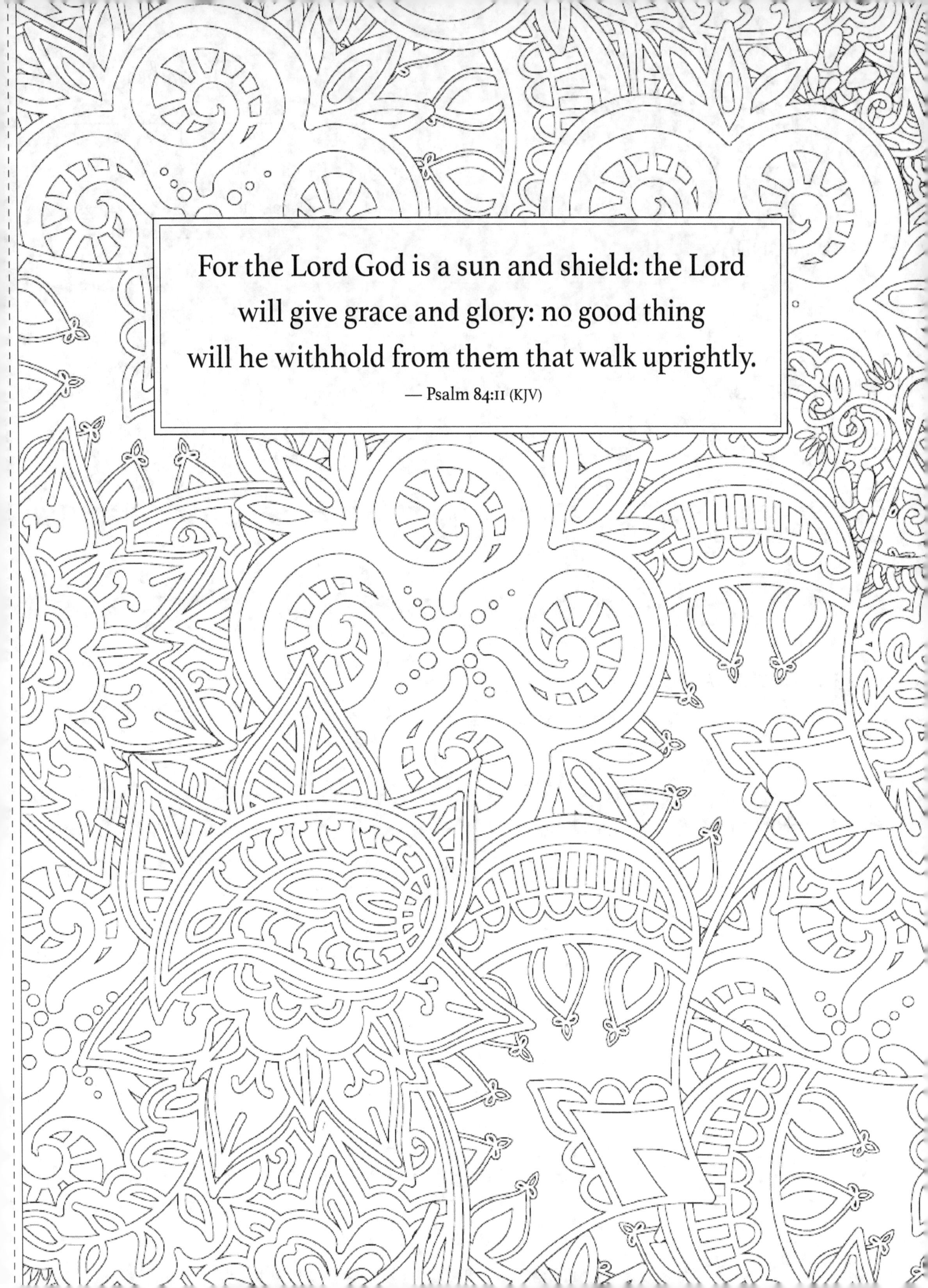

For the Lord God is a sun and shield: the Lord
will give grace and glory: no good thing
will he withhold from them that walk uprightly.
— Psalm 84:11 (KJV)

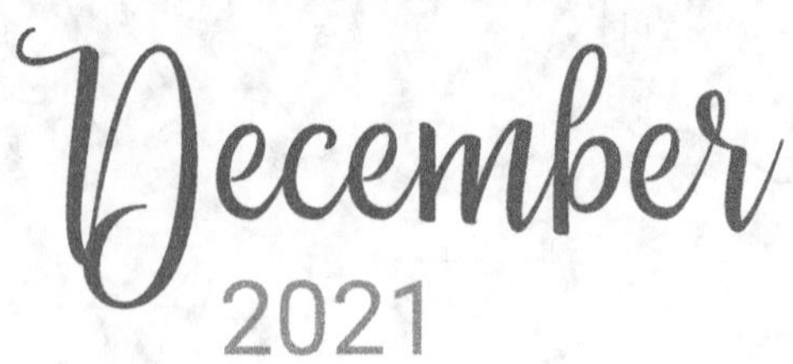

December
2021

13 MONDAY

14 TUESDAY

15 WEDNESDAY

16 THURSDAY

17 FRIDAY

18 SATURDAY

19 SUNDAY

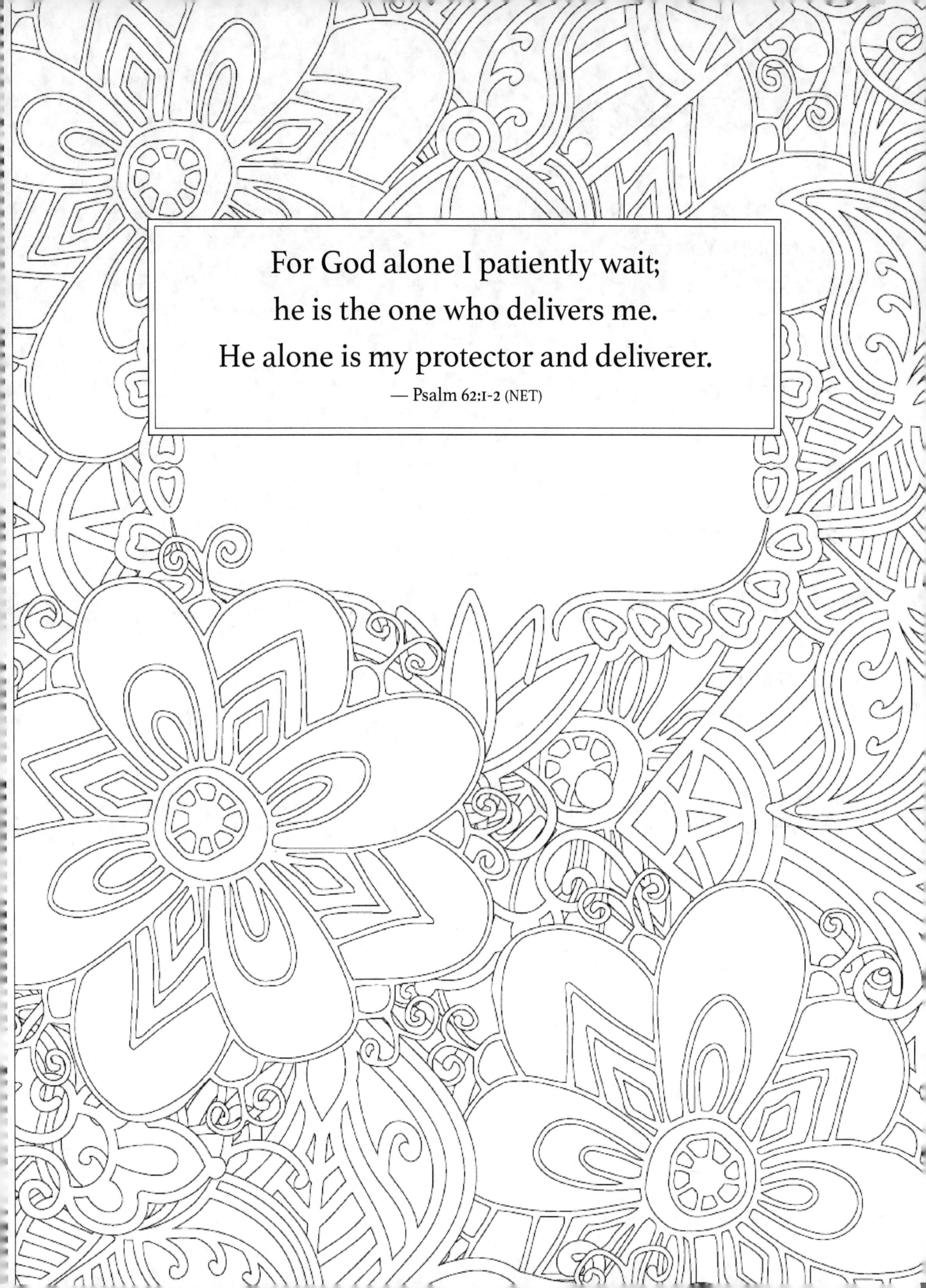

For God alone I patiently wait;
he is the one who delivers me.
He alone is my protector and deliverer.
— Psalm 62:1-2 (NET)

December
2021

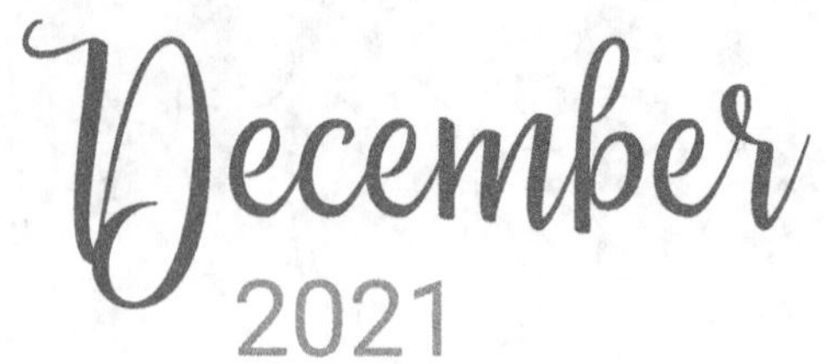

20 MONDAY

21 TUESDAY   First Day of Winter

22 WEDNESDAY

23 THURSDAY

24 FRIDAY   Christmas Eve

25 SATURDAY   Christmas Day

26 SUNDAY

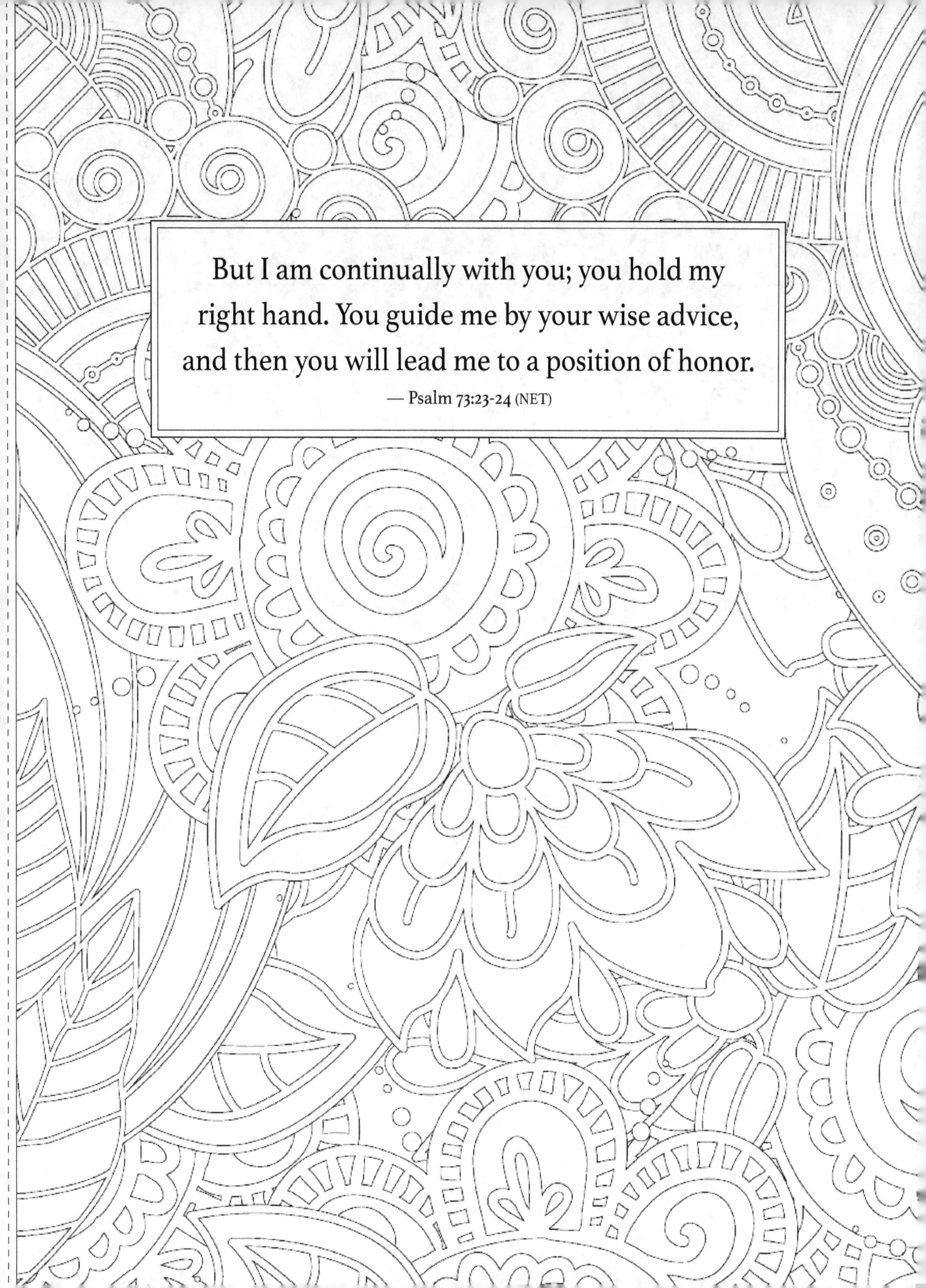

But I am continually with you; you hold my
right hand. You guide me by your wise advice,
and then you will lead me to a position of honor.
— Psalm 73:23-24 (NET)

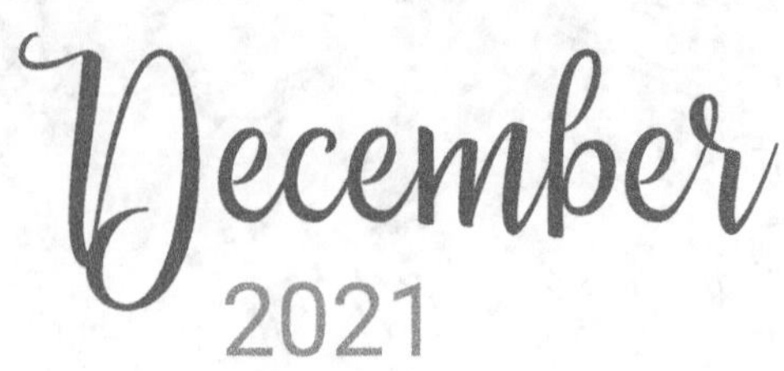

December
2021

27 MONDAY

28 TUESDAY

29 WEDNESDAY

30 THURSDAY

31 FRIDAY   New Year's Eve

01 SATURDAY   New Year's Day

02 SUNDAY

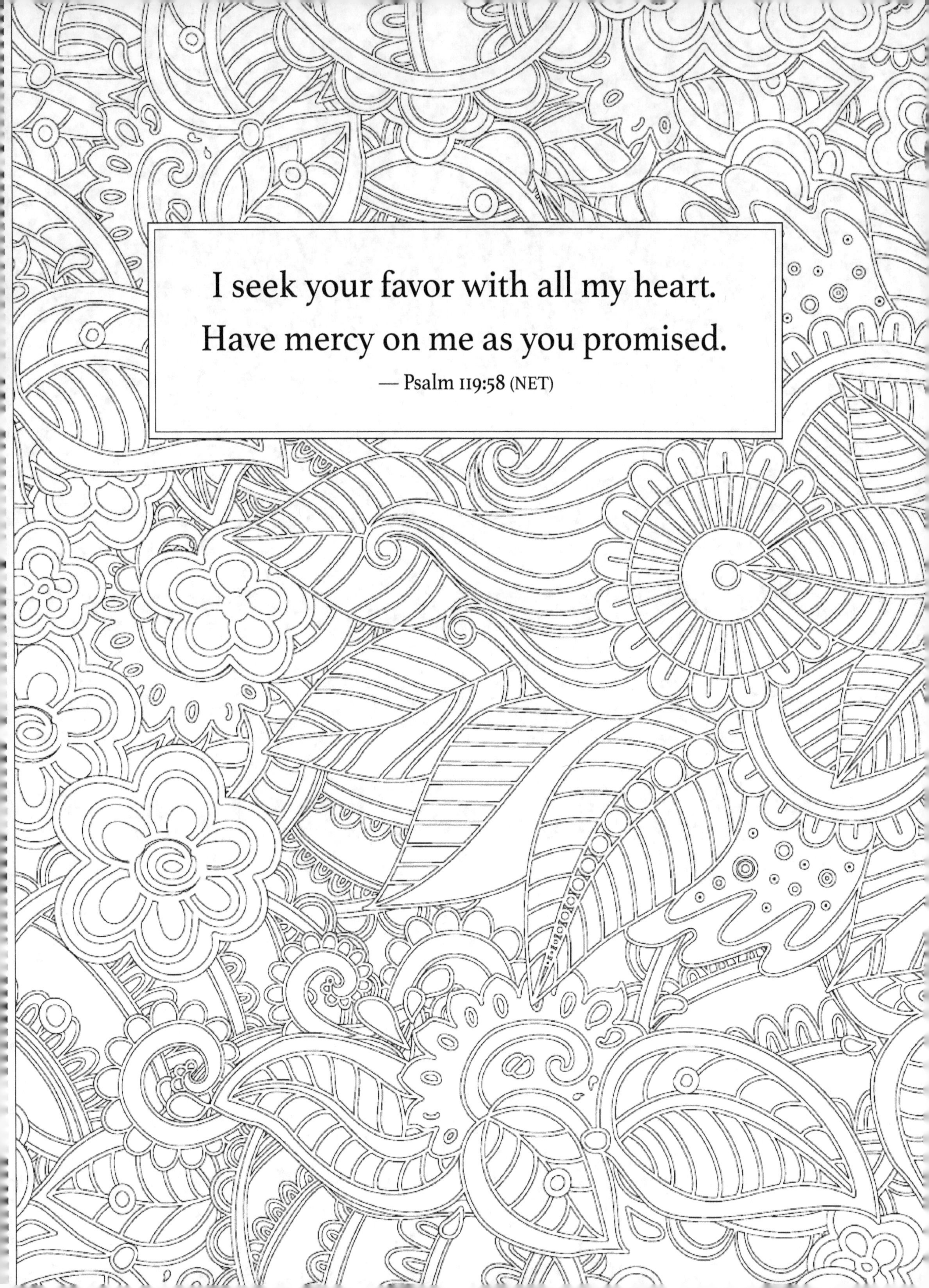

I seek your favor with all my heart.

Have mercy on me as you promised.

— Psalm 119:58 (NET)